WORKING WITH REFUGEES AND ASYLUM-SEEKERS

A Social Work Resource Book

by

Ruth Torode, Trish Walsh, Marguerite Woods

with

Treasa Galvin and Anna Fiona Keogh

Published by Department of Social Studies, Trinity College, Dublin 2, Ireland

ACKNOWLEDGEMENTS

We gratefully acknowledge the positive support and grant aid given by the Department of Justice, Equality and Law Reform Policy Planning Research Unit for the preparation of this training and resource pack for social workers and other professionals working with refugees and asylum-seekers.

Warm thanks are also due to:

Our colleagues in the Department of Social Studies, Trinity College - in particular to Robbie Gilligan and Eoin O'Sullivan - and to our former colleague, Caroline Skehill, who was involved in the early planning stage – for their advice and support.

Treasa Galvin in the Department of Sociology, Trinity College, who contributed Chapter Three, and was unfailingly helpful and encouraging about the project.

Anna-Fiona Keogh, who contributed Chapter Two, for her enthusiasm and support.

Deirdre McLoughlin, who acted as an exemplary research assistant in the summer and autumn of 1999, conducting interviews with practitioners and gathering information on other services.

To the professionals who generously agreed to be interviewed, often at considerable length, and whose observations and experience inform Chapter Four, but who remain anonymous.

To all the individuals and organisations who provided information and photographs for this project.

Department of Social Studies, Trinity College, Dublin 2, Ireland
2001
ISBN : 0-9515768-7-9

Design and production: Reprint Limited

CONTENTS

INTRODUCTION

In our work as educators on professional social work and addiction studies courses, the question of how best to integrate teaching and learning about principles and practice is an ongoing topic. It is one thing to promote ethical principles of equality and inclusiveness, but quite another to test and implement these principles in complex practice situations, where there are conflicts of interest, and where the information and resources needed for good practice may be lacking.

In this resource book, we have aimed to assemble some of the ingredients needed to underpin the integration of principles and practice in work with Refugees and Asylum-Seekers.

◆ Chapter One reviews the development and core concepts of a number of theoretical frameworks relevant to social work practice with oppressed minorities, in particular, anti-oppressive practice, multiculturalism and interculturalism, human rights and citizenship frameworks.

◆ Chapter Two provides an overview of the international and Irish legal and policy context for the reception of refugees and asylum seekers.

◆ Chapter Three explores the social circumstances of refugees and asylum seekers in Ireland, as they move from reception, through asylum application and adjudication, to departure or resettlement. Scenarios are included to stimulate exploration of the experience of being a refugee.

◆ Chapter Four explores some of the challenges, such as language, cultural differences, resource and coordination deficits, which confront Irish professionals offering services to refugees and asylum-seekers. Brief practice guidelines are offered. Scenarios are included to prompt discussion of how workers and agencies can best adapt to their new service users.

◆ Chapter Five draws together themes addressed in the preceding chapters and outlines a framework for applying anti-discriminatory and inclusive practice at two levels, those of the individual worker and the organisation.

◆ Chapter Six provides a resource list of organisations currently providing advice and support services for refugees and asylum-seekers.

Each of the first five chapters includes a guide to key reading.

The idea for the resource book was prompted by a number of developments over the past few years:

◆ An increasing emphasis in social work and other professional courses on inequalities and discrimination experienced by members of diverse minority groups.

◆ An increasing focus in training on frameworks for anti-oppressive practice and human rights as a challenge to and a resource for practitioners.

◆ The increasing number and visibility of Asylum-seekers arriving in Ireland, and the need to prepare students to work with this diverse new community.

◆ An increase in racist discourses about asylum-seekers and economic migrants, and the need to arm students with information and opportunities to address these discourses in a reflective manner.

It was gratifying that the Department of Justice, Equality and Law Reform Policy, Planning and Research Unit responded so positively to our proposal to develop curriculum material in this area.

Work began on the resource book in 1999 and interviews were conducted with a number of practitioners on the frontline of statutory and voluntary services for refugees and asylum-seekers.   In the period since then, many developments in policy and services for refugees and asylum-seekers have taken place very rapidly.   In some cases, difficulties mentioned by our interviewees have been partially addressed – for example, by the formation of a team of social workers to work with unaccompanied refugee minors. Numerous new publications and research projects have emerged, including some important Irish materials, to fill the gap in information.

Despite these rapid developments, and our experience of writing about policy and practice which were so soon superceded, we hope this resource book will provide a useful foundation for students and for others who wish to familiarise themselves with the circumstances of refugees and asylum seekers and with principles and guidelines for culturally sensitive practice.

Ruth Torode, Trish Walsh and Marguerite Woods.
May 2001.

CHAPTER ONE

PERSPECTIVES AND FRAMEWORKS FOR WORKING WITH MINORITIES

Introduction

Social work as a profession has always had as one of its defining properties a central concern with notions of social justice and equality and a commitment to serving oppressed populations. As professionals, we are expected to draw on a specific knowledge base in a conscious determination of a particular course of action to be taken with service users. The professional social worker is expected to:

act deliberately, taking the steps that are likely to be most helpful, least intrusive, and most consistent with the person's welfare (Mallon, 1998: 2).

It is important to remember that as social workers, we draw not only on knowledge derived from books or curriculum material, but also on many other forms of 'knowledge' in deciding what to do in practice with our clients. Mattaini (1995) has identified seven different sources and types of knowledge that form the base for social work practice and that are relevant for work with particular oppressed populations. They are:

◆ practice wisdom derived from narrative experiences of the profession and professional colleagues
◆ personal experience of the practitioner
◆ knowledge of the professional literature
◆ knowledge of history and current events
◆ research findings that inform practice
◆ theoretical and conceptual analyses
◆ information that is provided by the case itself.

This chapter addresses the professional literature and offers a conceptual and theoretical analysis of the different perspectives which inform social work practice with oppressed populations internationally. In considering the relevance of these approaches to Irish social work practice with oppressed populations, it is necessary to bear in mind both the uniqueness of the historical development of social work in Ireland (Skehill, 1999), and the distinctive Irish perception and treatment of specific oppressed populations over time.

As individuals, we bring to our social work practice the values, attitudes, beliefs and prejudices that we have acquired as members of the wider society. It is important to recognise our existing attitudes and beliefs, and then to consider how they may impact on our practice with others.

It is necessary therefore to look first at the 'popular' models which

Accessing Irish Society: Access Ireland Trainees. Dublin, 1999.
Photographer: Ann Moroney

eight

Solidarity: Participants at an Irish Traveller Movement rally to mark the 50th anniversary of the Universal Declaration of Human Rights. Dublin, December 1998   *Photographer : Derek Speirs / Report*

encapsulate general understandings and perceptions of minority groups, before moving to the 'professional' models of practice with these groups.

'Popular' Models for understanding the experience of minority groups

The Dublin Travellers Education and Development Group (DTEDG) has identified five different theoretical models which are used by the general population, or 'dominant cultural group' in their understanding of the Irish Traveller's situation. These are generic models which can be usefully employed to consider perceptions the dominant cultural group may have of other minority groups, such as refugees and asylum-seekers. It is important to consider these models, as all of us, as members of the general population, have been exposed to, and have absorbed, some of these dominant assumptions or beliefs.

> *Sometimes these perceptions are held explicitly and consciously, at other times they are implicit in what people say or write about travellers. They also become visible in the relations between sedentary people and Travellers or in the interventions of the State. A statement or slogan sums up the assumptions of each model, which we categorise as follows: liberal humanist, social pathology, subculture of poverty, idealist and human rights.* (O'Connell, 1994:11).

The Liberal Humanist model is defined by O'Connell as one which views 'Travellers as **individuals who are no different from anybody else',** but it is a perspective which has both positive and negative effects.

As O'Connell points out, when viewing 'Travellers as individuals who are no different from anybody else' implies that Travellers are equal citizens, it has a positive effect. This view can, however, also imply that Travellers have no distinct identity or culture, and so deny the real differences that exist between Travellers and sedentary people. In treating each person as an individual, the liberal humanist model ignores or minimises significant differences in people's individual experiences, such as race, class, and gender. In O'Connell's view, this orientation:

> *encourages the notion that Travellers should live in accordance with the expectations of sedentary people. When they refuse they are seen as failures or a social nuisance. This perception assumes that individual identity and sense of self are prior to and relatively independent of group membership. When individuals experience discrimination (social exclusion) because others recognise them as members of the Traveller community, then group membership is blamed for causing the oppression and structural patterns of group privilege and oppression are ignored. This individualistic approach cannot facilitate Travellers' self-determination.* (O'Connell, 1994: 11)

The liberal humanist perspective can be criticised on two fronts: firstly because, in this model, identities are presumed to develop on an individual and personal level; this denies the social construction of identity, whereby different identities are promoted or suppressed according to the self-interests of the dominant social order; and secondly because liberalism itself operates as an instrument of social control, with differing identities offered varying degrees of acceptance within the dominant social order - for example, some would argue that in Ireland in the early 21st century, refugees have achieved a level of social acceptability which is still denied to Irish Travellers.

The Social Pathology model views those who are from minority groups as deviants: **'Travellers are social misfits and drop-outs'.** Minority individuals and groups are seen as a problem and mainstream society is seen as unproblematic.

Drawing on the work of Paulo Freire (1978, 1982) and other theorists who have written about perceptions of oppressed populations, this model emphasises individual deviation from a societal norm, where the oppressed are regarded as the pathology of the healthy society. Those who are viewed as social misfits are therefore seen as responsible for their marginalisation and discrimination, or are viewed as 'victims' in need of charity. Personal inadequacy, a group-wide inability to function adequately, or 'vice', are cited as factors in the marginalisation process. Mainstream society is viewed as just and harmonious, and social misfits are viewed as socially pathological and in need of treatment. This focus on the deficits of the marginalised group means that issues of economic injustice, power imbalance, exploitation and oppression need not be explored. This leads to avoidance of the prejudice of the dominant groups in society and allows for the expression of negative stereotypes and racism.

O'Connell (1994) believes that, while this model is usually associated with right-wing groups, it has in Ireland also been evident among those on the political left who believe that Travellers are the lumpen-proletariat. Efforts have concentrated both on measures of social control, such as eviction or forced settlement with a view to assimilation, and on measures concerned with helping or doing something 'for' Travellers, such as the provision of rehabilitation techniques or services which are also intended to achieve assimilation by minimising the differences between Travellers and others, but which often perpetuate dependency.

O'Connell argues that the social pathology model is unable to account for the specific characteristics of different marginalised groups. In the case of Travellers, how are the various components of their identity - their historical development, the resilience of the population in the face of institutionalised prejudice, their cultural traditions, language, values and nomadic way of life, accounted for in the social pathology model?

The third model is that of **The Sub-Culture of Poverty.** While accepting that minority groups have values and distinct ways of life, this model views these differences as emanating from economic poverty alone. This model

holds that Travellers, as a marginalised group, pass on values and attitudes from one generation to the next which perpetuate poverty. (O'Connell, 1994: 13)

These values and attitudes, in the case of Travellers, are seen to privilege

a present-time orientation and an inability to defer gratification, thus making this population psychologically incapable of adapting to changing circumstances or new opportunities. This model assumes that the differences evident between mainstream society and minority groups emanate from the effects of poverty. The sub-culture of poverty therefore acts as a pattern which maintains the members of that community passively tied into a different way of being.

This model, however, is unable to account for the significant differences in economic power and resources which occur within particular populations, or the adaptability and ingenuity which has been evident among different oppressed groups such as Travellers and Refugees. The assumption that Irish Travellers are unable to defer gratification is a negative attribution, which reflects lack of adequate resources more than specific psychological problems or patterns.

Interventions with marginalised groups under this model are, like those of the liberal humanist and social pathology models, focused on assimilating the members of the minority group into mainstream society, and ignoring or erasing the differences between the different groups. Under the assimilation model, differences are not to be valued and preserved but to be eliminated.

The Idealist Model, in contrast to the first three models, views those from minority groups as 'special' and 'exotic'. In the case of Travellers, it can be summarised in the slogan: **'Envy those colourful Travellers wandering the rainbows of Ireland'**. (O'Connell, 1994: 14)

This model views members of minority groups as having some special innate quantities which mark them as different from 'ordinary' people, with a special status which needs to be protected. O'Connell notes that:

> *at its most simplistic and naive, this portrays all Travellers as having 'special' innate positive qualities. A more sophisticated variant explains Travellers' lives through their culture. Travellers are idealised and treated as if everything they say must be accurate or as if they possess some secret wisdom and knowledge. When it becomes obvious that Travellers are a group of ordinary people and make mistakes like everybody else then they fall from the pedestal and the idealist becomes disillusioned.* (O'Connell, 1994: 14)

This model, which is seen to be one of 'cultural reductionism', ignores the oppression that minority groups suffer and does not acknowledge the effects on a population of internalised oppression. Because of the 'special' label that is attached to the minority group, relationships are more likely to be patronising than equal.

The fifth model, **the Human Rights Model,** defines minority groups according to the features of the group which constitute a difference or grounds for discrimination under human rights legislation, such as sexual orientation, gender, ethnicity, disability, marital status. Under this model for example, 'Travellers are a nomadic ethnic group'. Under the human rights model, both differences in identity and experiences of discrimination are acknowledged as factors which contribute to the groups's marginalisation. Travellers, for instance, are viewed as an identifiable minority ethnic group since they regard themselves and are regarded by others as a people with distinct characteristics, including a long shared history, values, customs, lifestyle and traditions associated with nomadism. They are also seen as a small minority who share a history of oppression and discrimination. In the case of Irish Travellers, O'Connell has linked Travellers' developing consciousness of the root causes of their oppression with a strengthened sense of ethnicity.

The main disadvantage of the emphasis on ethnicity is that it can lead to a perception that those from ethnic groups are different, less equal, or less 'normal', by those from the dominant social order. This can develop into a mistaken assumption that ethnicity refers to some permanent essence attached to minorities that determines an individual's actions. This assumption needs to be counteracted by an emphasis on the difficulties of using one set of cultural norms - those of the dominant social order - to assess or judge the actions, behaviours and beliefs of another group with their own set of cultural norms. It is not saying that the dominant order or the minority order is either right or superior, but that there are difficulties in measuring those in minority groups by the standards and norms set by the dominant group. This is known as the 'cultural relativism' argument and leads to an encouragement for minority groups to take control of their own definitions and to engage in a dialogue with the dominant group about the cultural differences between them.

Discussion Points:

1.   How would Refugees and Asylum-Seekers be viewed under each of the five models?

2.   Which of these five models, in your opinion, offers the least discriminatory and most empowering perspective for understanding the experiences of minority groups?

Frameworks for Social Work Practice

Broadly speaking, there are five different perspectives which are drawn on by social workers in their direct practice with oppressed populations:

◆ Anti-racism
◆ Anti-oppressive / anti-discriminatory practice
◆ Interculturalism / Multiculturalism
◆ Human rights
◆ Social exclusion / Citizenship.

ANTI-RACISM

Anti-racism seeks to challenge racism as a key form of oppression which, connected to gender and class oppression, serves to limit the life chances and opportunities available to black children and their families...Antiracist social work means developing a model of strength and empowerment in social work. It is based on the self-definition of black experience, needs and aspirations and therefore involves the acknowledgement of black people's views, values and concerns. It involves dismantling pathological assumptions and cultural stereotypes in favour of an approach that is sensitive to cultural pride and differences. It requires a challenge to social work theories which are based on ethnocentric values and also a commitment to combating racism in all its forms. Antiracist social work involves an awareness of the processes and manifestations of racism; as well as understanding the power relationship between black and white people, it also requires an understanding of the power relationship of social worker/client. It means shifting from individual-focussed casework to the holistic approach favoured by black people, which does not treat people as though they existed in a vacuum but as part of a family, which is, in turn, part of the extended family and community (this does not mean ignoring the needs of individuals). Antiracist social work is not about non-intervention, it is about analysing the type of intervention and being mindful of the effects of the intervention. As racism can be measured by its effects, so antiracism can be measured by its outcomes, which are about utilising and building on people's strengths. (Gambe et al, 1992: 1-2)

This perspective in social work was developed primarily in the U.K., where concepts of 'race', racism and anti-racism characterised the debate about ethnic minorities. The British social and political context, at the time that this debate first surfaced in the 1960's and 1970's, was one of an established pattern of immigration into Britain from the Commonwealth countries. By the 1980's, when the debate about racism became central in social work discourse, it reflected an evident 'new racism' which developed

as the white Anglo-Saxon British response to Britain's declining socio-economic position and the existence of a substantial, settled, indigenous black population. (Dominelli, 1988:9).

The anti-racist perspective in social work developed in response to the failure of radical class-based theories to incorporate a black perspective in their analysis of the oppression of poverty.

Theorists such as Dominelli (1988; 1997) and Ahmad (1990) were central in developing the notion of 'anti-racist social work'. Dominelli defines racism as:

> *a set of practices which assumes the inherent superiority of one 'race' over others and thereby the right to dominate.. racism is about relations of dominance and subordination which are rooted in the 'othering' of others as a social process of exclusion in which particular personal attributes are identified as the basis for a racialised 'othering' to occur. These characteristics are aspects of an individual's or group's identity which are castigated as 'inferior' by a dominant group which has the power to enforce its definitions of reality on others.* (1998: 39)

Hence in this discourse, concepts of power, domination and subordination are central. The political processes through which dominant groups maintain their powerful position are not only acknowledged but seen to be of significant importance in the social worker's understanding of and action in the field of practice. Dominelli argues that a focus on practice without an accompanying understanding of context will:

> *omit discrimination which is perpetuated on a group of individuals, or even individual members of a disadvantaged group through practitioner intervention.* (1998: 43)

Dominelli constructed an anti-racist framework for social work practice, which emphasised that racism occurs at three different levels: the individual, institutional and cultural (1988). Consequently, social work practice and social work education need to start with a process of 'conscientisation' (Freire, 1970), by means of which

> *individuals make connections between the social relations they endorse and perpetuate through their attitudes, values and behaviour and the social positions they occupy.* (Dominelli, 1988: 71)

Social workers need to introduce change at both personal and institutional levels in order to alter individual conduct in interpersonal relations and to transform the allocation of power and resources in society.

Dominelli identified ten activities that need to be undertaken by social workers in order for a 'non-racist' practice to be developed:

◆ Change the current definition of the social work task to one which does not render oppression invisible.
◆ Negate the 'objectivity' currently embedded in the professionalism underpinning a status quo which has been found seriously wanting.
◆ Alter existing power relationships between service users and workers; the voice of the 'expert' should not substitute for that of the oppressed.

- ◆ Do not deny consumers their right to determine the types of welfare provisions on offer.
- ◆ Stop treating people's welfare, at both individual and group level, as a commodity that can be rationed for the purposes of controlling people and their aspirations; instead, it should enhance personal fulfilment and well-being.
- ◆ Change the basis of training, which assumes a false neutrality on major social and ethical issues of the day, to one making explicit its value base and taking a moral and political stance against oppression in any form.
- ◆ Terminate an allocation of power and resources which perpetuates injustice and misery and replace it with one committed to implementing justice and equality for all.
- ◆ End the theoretical separation between social work and a) other key elements of the state, especially welfare sectors, and b) the'law and order' apparatus including police and courts; instead the connections between each of these parts must be made visible.
- ◆ End the separation between policy and practice, exposing the connections between them.
- ◆ Replace the lack of political commitment to end racial inequality, with one operating in the opposite direction. (Dominelli, 1988: 162 - 163)

The anti-racist social work framework is, like all other theories, a product of its time, and has been influential in the field of social work practice and education in the U.K. during the 1980s and 1990s. It has challenged social workers to acknowledge: the oppressiveness of a colour-blind approach to work with ethnic minorities; the limitations of a casework or individual focus in the face of structural inequalities; and the importance of understanding the effects of racism and discrimination on ethnic minorities. It has also attracted critics who have argued against what came to be seen as a 'politically correct' practice, which concentrated too much on selective oppressions, such as racism and sexism, to the detriment of other wider oppressions, such as poverty and inequality of opportunity.

There have also been fears that too strong an emphasis on 'anti-racist awareness training' has not enabled social work practitioners and students to de-construct their own attitudes and beliefs in a positive atmosphere, but may have led to negative attitudes going underground instead.

The anti-racist perspective, while still of value in relation to the specific needs of ethnic minorities, has been subsumed by the more generic anti-discriminatory and anti-oppressive frameworks which evolved from it.

Key Readings

Dominelli, L. (1988), *Anti-Racist Social Work.* London: Macmillan/BASW.

Dominelli, L. (1997), *Anti-Racist Social Work.* Second edition. London:Macmillan /BASW.

Dominelli, L. (1998) *Multiculturalism, Anti-Racism and Social Work.* in Williams, Soydan and Johnson (eds.) *Social Work and Minorities: European perspectives.* London: Routledge.

Gambe, D. Gomes, J, Kapur, V, Rangel, M, Stubbs, P. (1992), *Antiracist Social Work Education, 2: Improving Practice with Children and Families: A Training Manual.* London: CCETSW.

Anti-Oppressive / Anti-Discriminatory Practice (AOP/ADP)

Anti-discriminatory practice

> *is an approach to social work practice which seeks to reduce, undermine or eliminate discrimination and oppression, specifically in terms of challenging sexism, racism, ageism and disabilism and other forms of discrimination encountered in social work. Social workers occupy positions of power and influence, and so there is considerable scope for discrimination and oppression, whether this is intentional or by default. Anti-discriminatory practice is an attempt to eradicate discrimination from our own practice and challenge it in the practice of others and the institutional structures in which we operate.*
> (Thompson,1993: 31- 32)

A product of the 1990s, anti-discriminatory practice is an approach, like anti-oppressive practice (Dalrymple and Burke, 1995), which includes all forms of oppression in a generic anti-discriminatory framework. Oppression is defined as:

> *Inhuman or degrading treatment of individuals or groups; hardship and injustice brought about by the dominance of one group over another; the negative and demeaning exercise of power.* (Thompson, 1993: 31)

Both frameworks start from the view that social work practice which ignores oppression and discrimination cannot be seen as good practice. Like the anti-racist model, both frameworks were developed in the context of British social work and have shared roots in radical social work, feminist theory and anti-racist and black perspectives. Payne notes that these approaches

> *arose from the needs of agencies and workers facing new ethnic issues, spurring them on to reform by rising conflicts.* (1997: 248)

The most distinctive feature of these approaches, in comparison to the multi-cultural or pluralist frameworks, is their primary focus on structural inequalities in society.

Both ADP and AOP make an analysis of discrimination which links the personal, cultural and societal levels.

> *Dalrymple and Burke's analysis... develops a practice model involving the worker and client in a partnership committed to change in order to achieve greater equality in society. This operates at the level of feelings, reflecting the client's and worker's biographies, at the level of ideas, working to achieve a changed consciousness of both feelings and society and at the level of political action in wider society.* (Payne, 1997: 245)

Oppression is not a mono-dimensional concept but one which acknowledges

> *multiple oppression - the interaction of various sources and forms of oppression (where) oppression and discrimination are presented as aspects of the divisive nature of social structure - reflections of the social divisions of class, gender, age, disability and sexual orientation* (Thompson, 1993: 11).

Various forms of oppression are seen to have an impact on individual and collective identity, in terms of: alienation, isolation, marginalisation, economic position and life-chances, confidence and self-esteem, and social expectations and career opportunities.

Thompson (1993) also examines other forms of oppression, such as those based on religion (sectarianism), sexual orientation (heterosexism), and 'cultural hegemony' - whereby one group maintains dominance over another through the oppression of cultural or linguistic minorities.

Thompson, like Dominelli, identifies steps that need to be taken to further the anti-oppressive practice agenda:

◆ Much of the discrimination inherent in social work can be seen to be unintentional - due to a lack of awareness rather than deliberate attempts to oppress. For this reason, awareness training has a major part to play in challenging and confronting discrimination.
◆ Awareness training provides consciousness-raising for individuals, but its value can be multiplied by raised collective awareness and subsequent collective action. A collective response to examples of discrimination can have a much more potent effect than an individual response. In addition, each individual can act with greater confidence in the knowledge that there exists the backing of others within a collective anti-discriminatory project.
◆ Anti-discriminatory social work needs to be based on applying theory to practice. Anti-intellectual tendencies in social work exist, which devalue theory and advocate a 'common-sense' approach to social work, which is particularly dangerous for anti-discriminatory practice, because 'common-sense' actually amounts to a mixture of dominant ideologies - sexist, racist and so on. They are a collection of taken-for-granted assumptions which are likely to be discriminatory and oppressive in their content and impact. Instead, practice should be based on a clear and explicit theory base, in order to swim against the tide of dominant discriminatory assumptions.
◆ The development of anti-discriminatory practice requires location of the issues and principles as central to the practice of social work, and not as optional extras. Equality of opportunity should be a central feature of all social work theory, policy and practice.
◆ Individual practitioners need to remain open and critical in their practice, to ensure that it remains anti-discriminatory and anti oppressive. (Thompson, 1993)

One of the strengths of this perspective is that it emphasises similarities and continuities between the various forms of oppression which clients can experience, of which social workers need to develop awareness and counter-action. As a generic model, it is also more likely to be incorporated through general principles for practice than more specific theories.

Payne has outlined some difficulties associated with this AOP/ADP approach:

◆ These perspectives are a relatively recent theoretical development. It is as yet unclear whether they will prevail. They derive from a particular and basically structural analysis, such as that of radical and Marxist approaches. This analysis is not without controversy.

◆ Generic anti-discriminatory approaches view the interaction between various oppressions as complex. This can present practical and ideological problems, as agencies or workers may specialise in ways which makes it impossible for them to accord equal weight to all oppressions.

◆ Clients may resist attempts by workers to highlight or work on anti-discriminatory needs, if they have come for help with other needs.

Key Readings

Dalrymple, J. and Burke, B. (1995) *Anti-oppressive Practice: Social Care and the Law, Buckingham:* Open University Press.

Payne, M. (1997) *Modern Social Work Theory* Second edition. Chapter 11: "Anti-discriminatory and Anti-oppressive Perspectives". London: Macmillan.

Thompson, N. (1993) *Anti-discriminatory Practice,* London: Macmillan / BASW.

Thompson, N. (1997) *Anti-discriminatory Practice,* Second edition. London: Macmillan / BASW.

Interculturalism / Multiculturalism

Interculturalism or Multiculturalism is a perspective for work with minority groups which emphasises the importance of practitioners becoming 'culturally competent' in their dealings with minority groups. In its more recent formulation – interculturalism – it emphasises the process of interaction between different cultural groups and suggests the concept of cultural fusion in multicultural societies.

The ideal of multiculturalism

embraces notions of tolerance between individuals and social groups.
(Soydan and Williams,1998: 10)

But whether this ideal can realistically be achieved has been questioned (Nowak, 1997); and whether, as a liberal principle, it merely disguises major inequalities and intolerance has been suggested (Soydan and Williams, 1998). Tolerance, as a concept in itself, the same authors suggest, implies that there is something intrinsically objectionable to tolerate, and can lead to paternalism, with which multiculturalism has been said to have become associated.

The concept of multiculturalism has been defined in many different ways. More recent definitions go beyond ethnic and racial difference to include gender, socio-economic status, sexual orientation, age, religious affiliation, and physical and mental disabilities. One such definition has defined culture to include demographic variables, such as age and sex; status variables, such as social and economic status; affiliations, both formal and informal; as well as ethnographic variables, such as language, religion, nationality and ethnicity. (Pedersen, 1991)

In an early work, multiculturalism was defined as:

that state in which one has mastered the knowledge and developed the skills necessary to feel comfortable and communicate effectively (1) with people of any culture encountered, and (2) in any situation involving a group of people of diverse cultural backgrounds. By comfortable we mean without the anxiety, defensiveness and disorientation that usually accompany the initial intercultural experience. The multicultural person is the person who has learned how to learn culture - rapidly and effectively. (Hoopes, 1979: 21, cited in Ronnau, 1994: 31)

Originating in North America, the multicultural model focused primarily on educating workers in the human services to become more culturally aware and culturally sensitive in a social context comprising large groups of recent immigrants and an indigenous native American population, with specific language, cultural and practical issues.

The concepts and procedures in this approach are:

derived from the assumption that knowledge, understanding, acceptance, and sensitivity to cultural and human diversity are prerequisites for effective work with clients of diverse social and cultural backgrounds. (Chau, 1990: 124-125)

Multiculturalism emphasises the importance of

◆ raising awareness
◆ developing knowledge
◆ creating environments within which information sharing and questioning can safely take place.

Chau's (1990) model for cross-cultural practice in social work makes an important distinction between the concepts of cultural pluralism and cultural ethnocentrism.

Cultural pluralism:

embraces a mutual respect for the existence of cultural differences among racial and ethnic groups and recognises the cultural strengths inherent in those differences....supports the rights of different racial and ethnic groups to maintain their uniqueness while they contribute to the American culture, making the whole richer than the parts. (Chau, 1990: 125)

Cultural ethnocentrism:

views the mainstream culture as superior to ethnic cultures...advocates the perpetuation of mainstream culture and values as the single standard against which the merits of other groups are gauged. (Chau, 1990: 125)

Chau suggests that these two concepts can be seen as opposite ends of a values continuum for viewing ethnic diversity and cultural differences in our clients. Chau also draws on the concept of 'sociocultural dissonance', which he uses to refer to 'the stress and strain of cultural incongruence, and to the internal conflict caused by the social and cultural ramifications of being different'. Socio-cultural dissonance occurs when

minorities seek to cope with their life situations while under the pressure to conform to the dual, often conflicting or incongruent requirements of both minority and dominant cultural systems. (Chau, 1990: 126).

This dissonance is seen to arise from the dual perspective which people from minority groups have to adopt - as they live not only in the dominant cultural environment subjected to its influences, but are also embedded in their own cultural environment, which gives special meanings to the common life problems they face. Because of the variation in world views, values and cultural beliefs, a degree of incongruence can exist between the norms and expectations of the two cultural environments. The degree of incongruence can vary depending on the level of bi-culturation an individual accomplishes.

Chau proposes a cross-cultural practice model for social work, which rests on two axes: one represents the ideological value continuum of ethnocentrism and pluralism; the other defines the targets or goals of intervention on a continuum from individual change to sociostructural change.

Multiculturalism, as an example of a pluralist approach, has been criticised for focusing too much on the attitudinal aspect without sufficient regard to the wider frame - the institutional and sociostructural factors which perpetuate intolerance and prejudice (Harlow & Hearn, 1996). It has been seen in opposition to 'anti-racism' which emphasises structures and ideologies. Payne concludes that:

Simple pluralism in the 'race' field appears to have been defeated by the arguments for a structuralist position'. (Payne, 1997: 254)

Some recent American multicultural frameworks for practice, however, have embraced the wider dimension and have argued for the need to challenge the dominant culture and structural inequalities, as well as to develop skills and expertise in cross-cultural practice:

This model recognises the validity of minority cultures and aims to change the ways in which workers and agencies relate to minority groups. It aims to increase workers sensitivity to differing cultural norms, and to decrease institutional racism. Strategies such as providing training in cross-cultural competence, increasing minority participation in agencies and enacting equal rights legislation are employed. (Potocky, 1997: 318)

The most recent development within this framework is the development of 'Interculturalism', which emphasises the two-way process of communication between cultural groups. This challenges the one-way linear dynamic of the early multicultural literature, which exhorted practitioners from dominant cultures to become skilled in working with service users from other cultural groups.

Interculturalism has been adopted by many Irish organisations working with refugees and asylum-seekers, such as The National Consultative Committee on Racism and Multiculturalism, who define it in relation to their aims thus:

The promotion of a more participative and intercultural society which is more inclusive of groups such as refugees, Travellers, and other minority ethnic groups. (National Consultative Committee on Racism webpage: http://homepage.tinet.ie/~racismctee/)

Key Readings

Chau, K. (1990) "A Model for Teaching Cross-cultural Practice in Social Work", *Journal of Social Work Education,* 26.2. : 124 - 133.

Potocky, M. (1997) "Multicultural social work in the United States: a review and critique", *International Social Work,* 40 : 315 - 326.

Ronnau, J. (1994) "Teaching Cultural Competence: practical ideas for social work educators", *Journal of Multicultural Social Work,* 3.1 : 29 - 42.

Ewalt, P, Freeman, E, Kirk, S. and Poole, D. (eds.) (1996) *Multicultural Issues in Social Work,* Washington: NASW Press.

Vace, N, deVaney, S. and Wittmer, J. (1995) *Experiencing and Counselling Multicultural and diverse Populations* (Third edition), Bristol, PA: Accelerated Development Publishers.

Human Rights: transnational rights perspective

Human rights can be generally defined as those rights which are inherent in our nature and without which we cannot live as human beings. Human rights and fundamental freedoms allow us to fully develop and use our human qualities, our intelligence, our talents and our conscience and to satisfy our spiritual and other needs. They are based on mankind's increasing demand for a life in which the inherent dignity and worth of each human being will receive respect and protection. (UN, 1987: 4)

The historical development of the current concept of human rights is often traced from the eighteenth century, culminating in the American Declaration of Independence and the French Declaration of the Rights of Man. However, it is also clear that many of the core elements of human rights were present and enforced in western and non-western cultures and societies from ancient times.

The 'modern' development of human rights is seen to include three distinct phases:

◆ A concern for civil and political rights in the eighteenth century in Europe and America;
◆ An increasing demand for economic, social and cultural rights from the time of the Industrial Revolution, progressing more slowly and at varied rates in different parts of the world; and
◆ A third generation of rights which is currently being promoted - to peace, development and a clean environment protected from destruction. (UN Centre for Human Rights, 1994).

The aftermath of the First World War focused attention on the interdependency between nations, and momentum gathered for the creation of an institutional framework for international co-operation.

'The establishment of the League of Nations and the International Labour Organisation and the inception of social welfare organizations, such as the International Conference of Social Welfare, the International Committee of Schools of Social Work and the International Permanent Secretariat of Social Workers in the 1920s were evidence of this new mood of international, regional and national collaboration.' (UN, 1987: 7)

The Second World War was the stimulus for the next stage of development of human rights. The Universal Declaration of Human Rights was adopted by the United Nations General Assembly in 1948. It asserts that:

(The) recognition of the inherent dignity and of the equal and inalienable rights of all members of the human family is the foundation of freedom, justice and peace in the world. (UN, 1994:4)

Witkin (1998) notes that, after the atrocities of the Second World War, the international community was mobilised to make such a declaration, with the hope that its adoption by members states would help to ensure that further gross abuses of human rights could be avoided. The office of the United Nations High Commissioner for Human Rights was subsequently created, and is currently occupied by Mary Robinson, former President of Ireland.

Current Legislative Frameworks

Instruments providing general protection

◆ *Charter of the United Nations (1945)*
◆ *Universal Declaration of Human Rights (1948)*
◆ *International Covenants on Human Rights (1966)*

Instruments providing particular protection

◆ *International Convention of the Elimination of All Forms of Racial Discrimination (1965)*
◆ *Convention on the Elimination of All Forms of Discrimination Against Women (1979)*
◆ *Convention Against Torture and Other Inhuman or Degrading Treatment or Punishment (1984)*
◆ *Convention on the Rights of the Child (1989)*

European Frameworks

◆ *European Convention on Human Rights (1950)*
◆ *European Court of Human Rights (1970)*

Human Rights and Social Work

The human rights advocate maintains that human rights are universal and should apply to all persons without discrimination. Respect for individual rights needs to be upheld at all times, irrespective of circumstances or political systems. The rights of any particular individual or group in any particular circumstances can be restricted only if they threaten to curtail similar or comparable rights of others. Given the focus that social work has maintained on social justice, the concept of human rights is broadly in line with the core philosophical values of social work, particularly in relation to: value for life; freedom and liberty; equality and non-discrimination; justice, solidarity and social responsibility.

Social work is viewed by human rights activists as particularly important in the identification of, and work against, injustice and the deprivation of rights, because it operates at the interface between State and individual, often with particularly oppressed and marginalised groups:

Social workers work with their clients on a variety of levels: the micro level of individual and family; the meso level of community; and the macro level of society - nationally and internationally. Concern for human rights must be manifested by social workers at all levels and at all times. (UN Centre for Human Rights, 1994: 3)

The focus on human rights in the media and popular press tends to rest on gross abuses, for example, recent tragedies in Rwanda, Bosnia and Kosovo. There is a risk that we presume in the modern Western world that most human rights are already guaranteed to the majority of people. However, as Witkin (1998) has pointed out, many of the conditions which cause people to seek help from social workers are related to the consequences of oppression and injustice:

> *social work's concern for meeting basic human needs, its respect for differences, and its social change orientation position it at the forefront of human rights struggles.* (Witkin, 1998: 198).

The UN (1994) recommends that, from a human rights perspective, we consider the needs and rights of refugees and asylum-seekers in two ways:

(a) *Identify particular difficulties*
- ◆ Emergency measures in the first country of asylum; family reunion
- ◆ Psychological issues, including post-traumatic stress in refugee camps
- ◆ Special needs of refugee children
- ◆ Special needs of refugee women
- ◆ Security of person and socio-economic protection, including the right to work
- ◆ Preparation for resettlement
- ◆ Integration in country of resettlement
- ◆ Voluntary repatriation

(b) ***Analyse the wider context***

In analysing the problems that refugees and asylum-seekers face, the UN also recommends that workers consider the causes for the flight of individuals, families or large segments of the population from their country of origin. This is an important step, both in allowing individuals to tell their own stories, and also in providing a context for the individual stories that will be told. Showing understanding of, and willingness to learn about, conditions in countries of origin also demonstrate interest and commitment on the part of the worker. Such a stance also helps to ensure that workers' perceptions are based, not only on impressionistic and politicised accounts by the media, but also on information from more credible sources, such as the European and United Nations bodies which produce detailed and informative reports on human rights and refugee issues.

Most of the causes of refugee movement are easily detectable - such as war, persecution and conflict. However, it has been noted that

> *There appears to be a growing lack of political will to admit refugees on the part of countries of first asylum and countries of intended final destination.* (UN, 1994: 39)

and there is a case to be made for

> *preventative, economic and other action in countries of origin, which could possible help to ease tensions and thus avoid the exodus of nationals in search of refuge and asylum elsewhere.* (UN, 1994: 39)

It must be accepted that, until such time as Ireland and other wealthy nations provide such remedies closer to the centres of conflict, war and persecution, increases in numbers seeking asylum are likely to continue.

Witkin has pointed out that

> *our notions of human rights are tied to the kind of society we want (the good society) and the way people within that society would live (the good life). As a philosophical and moral concept, human rights are about what it means to be human and and the requisite requirements to live a life worthy of a human being. These same ideals distinguish social work as a helping profession that is grounded in a vision of a just society and the values associated with that society.* (Witkin, 1998: 200)

Witkin calls on social workers who adopt a human rights perspective in their work to create an 'egalitarian plateau' - a conceptual space, where we might find agreement on some basic principles of human rights, especially how they apply to social work, and where political differences can be argued, so that for social workers this egalitarian ideal and moral warrant can be used as a powerful force for social change.

Key Readings

Witkin, S. (1998), 'Human Rights and Social Work', *Social Work,* 43.3: 197-201.

United Nations Centre for Human Rights (1994) *Human Rights and Social Work - a Manual for Schools of Social Work and the Social Work Profession.* New York: United Nations Centre for Human Rights.

Citizenship and Social Exclusion

Social exclusion has been defined as a successor to the associated concepts of poverty and divided societies

which refers not only to material deprivation, but to the inability of the poor to fully exercise their social, cultural and political rights as citizens. (Powell, 1995: 23)

'*Social exclusion*' is a relatively modern concept, which has become particularly influential in the European context, and which has been linked by many to the concept of citizenship and the extent to which minority groups, and particularly immigrant and refugee populations, are awarded or denied citizenship within the European community.

Citizenship has been defined as consisting of 'a three-legged stool'.

First there are fundamental civil rights such as freedom of speech, thought and religious toleration; equality before the law, the due process of the justice system, the right to conclude contracts as equals - the rule of law in its broadest sense. Second, there are basic political rights including the right to vote, form political parties and contest elections - democratic pluralism in essence. Third, there are basic social rights - the whole range from the right to a modicum of economic welfare and security to the right to share to the full the social heritage and to live the life of a civilised being according to the standards of the prevailing society. (Powell, 1995: 23).

The development of social citizenship rights, in Powell's analysis, is the product of class struggle 'incrementally promoting an increasing egalitarian society for the majority', and has constituted one of the core ideas of the Welfare State. Its significance is that democratic participation within such Welfare States is based on the means of distribution - the Welfare State - rather than on the market economy.

In this political order, the State has achieved hegemony through regulating the relationship between labour and business and the redistributive systems involving taxation and social welfare benefits (Powell, 1995: 25).

In the Irish context, the development of the concept of 'social partnership' and the various Programmes which have been initiated between government, labour and business partners in the national interest, exemplifies this trend.

The case has been made by many commentators (Powell,1995; Duffy,1994; I.F.S.W.,1996), that developments which have promoted the rights of majority populations within democratic States have also produced an 'underclass' within such societies; this 'underclass' comprises not only groups such as lone parents, unemployed, disabled and older people, but also other minority groups, such as Travellers, people with HIV/AIDS, drug users, refugees and asylum-seekers, "*who experience social exclusion at its most extreme*". (Powell, 1995: 27)

Migration controls, and legislation relating to nationality and the rights of refugees, have been seen to have a disproportionate effect upon particular minorities within the European context.

> *The development of European-wide structures has, while creating a notionally 'common travel area' for free trade, generated barriers and difficulties for minorities and set limits upon the enjoyment of hard-won privileges or rights for those who are seen to be different.* (Johnson, Balwin-Edwards and Moraes, 1998: 59)

These authors further point out that the Rights of Citizenship outlined under European law appear to be limited to people holding nationality of a member State, and contain restrictions in relation to the awarding of citizenship to so-called 'third - country nationals'; thus:

> *non-citizens - 'guest workers', 'third-country nationals' or by whatever term they may be called - are even further marginalised and at risk.Those who appear to be 'in' but not 'of' Europe, according to the stereotypes and suspicions of State functionaries, may be exposed to the dangers of internal policing designed to reinforce the privileges of membership.* (Johnson, Balwin-Edwards and Moraes, 1998: 60)

Throughout Europe, countries are strengthening their common external borders, for example by increased visa controls and fines on airlines, whilst simultaneously establishing common criteria for the treatment of refugees and asylum-seekers - leading to the 'Fortress Europe' metaphor. However, as Johnson *et al* point out, these policies

> *have been completely one-sided, concentrating on crisis management of migrant flows....The effect of asymmetrical policy creation - that is, control of immigrants without a corresponding development of immigrants' rights - has been to modernise immigration policy at the cost of dehumanising it.* (ibid,1998: 71)

The International Federation of Social Workers European Secretariat received funding in the early 1990's to develop policy in relation to the fight against exclusion. Social workers are seen to be central in the fight against social exclusion because:

◆ They have in-depth knowledge of the factors which push people into situations, where they need re-socialisation, re-integration and rehabilitation.
◆ They are equipped with the expertise to offer preventative services and interventions.
◆ Social workers can identify the marginalised and socially excluded minorities who find it difficult to access services, and actively seek them out.
◆ Social workers encourage service users to participate in the planning, implementation and improvement of a service.
◆ Social workers have an integrated view of problems, and can draw on the expertise of specialised professions where necessary. The different skills which social workers offer - such as the combination of counselling with practical assistance, and knowledge of organisations, means that they can co-ordinate a range of service agencies and

professions.

◆ Central to social work is the integrity of each individual's goals and ambitions. Social work support allows clients the space to make their own choices and express themselves (I.F.S.W., 1996).

Key Readings

Duffy, C. (1994) "Female Poverty, Powerlessness and Social Exclusion in Ireland", *Administration, 42.1: 47 - 66.*

I.F.S.W. (1996) *Fighting Exclusion: social work in action.* Promotional leaflet.

Johnson, M., Baldwin-Edwards, M. and Moraes, C. (1998) "Controls, rights and migration" in Williams, C. et al, *Social Work with Minorities.* London: Routledge.

Powell, F. (1995) "Citizenship and Social Exclusion", *Administration,* 43.3 : 22-35

CHAPTER 2

LEGAL CONTEXT

This chapter is concerned with legal provision for refugees and asylum-seekers. It will briefly review the history of international and Irish responses to, and development of policies and laws for, refugees and asylum seekers. It will also outline recent changes in policy and legislation introduced in response to the increased number of refugees and asylum-seekers in Ireland.

Introduction

The existence of refugees and asylum-seekers is a global issue. It may be thought that the European Union (EU) and the West provide for the majority of the world's refugees, but in fact, Europe and North America receive less than 10% of the world's refugees. According to the UNHCR, the total population of concern - refugees and displaced people world wide - at the start of the new millennium was 22.3 million, "or one out of every 269 persons on Earth". Refugees numbered 11.7 million. In 1998, Asia hosted the highest number of refugees (41%); Africa hosted 28%; Europe 23%; North America (6%); and the Caribbean and Oceania 1%. The majority of all refugees and displaced people are female. (UNHCR website: www.unhcr.ch)

Most refugees do not seek asylum in the EU or North America but in their neighbouring countries. So it is mainly developing countries that host the world's refugees. Although the West may seem a tempting place to seek asylum, there are many practical difficulties which deter refugees from seeking asylum there, including lack of transport, scarcity of funds, difficulty in obtaining official identity and travel documents, and a wide-spread recognition that asylum is difficult to gain in Western countries.

The existence of refugees and asylum seekers is not only a global but also an ancient phenomenon. As long as there has been war, persecution of social groups and abuses of human rights, there have been refugees. It was only in the twentieth century, however, that a co-ordinated international response to the plight of refugees was instrumented.

Development of International Policies

The first international instrument, which aimed to define and respond to refugees, was the United Nations Geneva Convention relating to the Status of Refugees in 1951. It had its roots in international efforts to respond to refugees of the First World War, the Russian Revolution, the Spanish Civil War and the rise of fascist dictatorships in Europe prior to the Second World War. Agreements developed before the Second World War were designed to respond to refugees within a specific historical and territorial context: that is to say, refugees were defined by a particular event in a particular country.

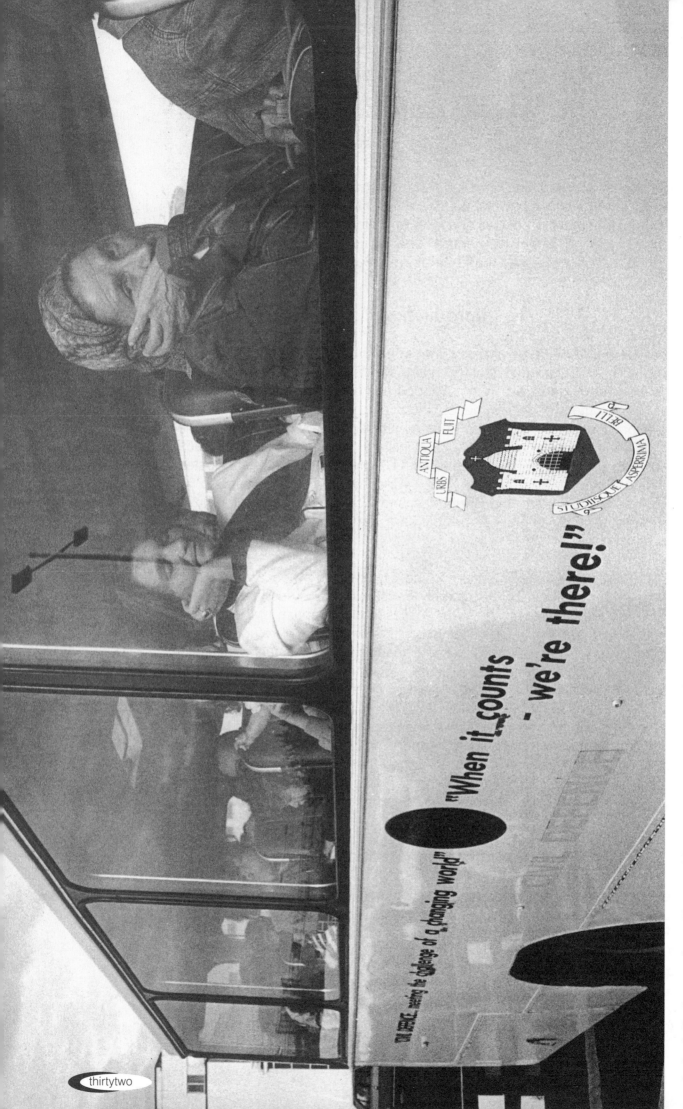

Arrival: Refugees from Former Yugoslavia travelling on a Civil Defence Bus from Dublin Airportto Cherry Orchard Hospital, Dublin. September 1992
Photographer: Derek Speirs / Report

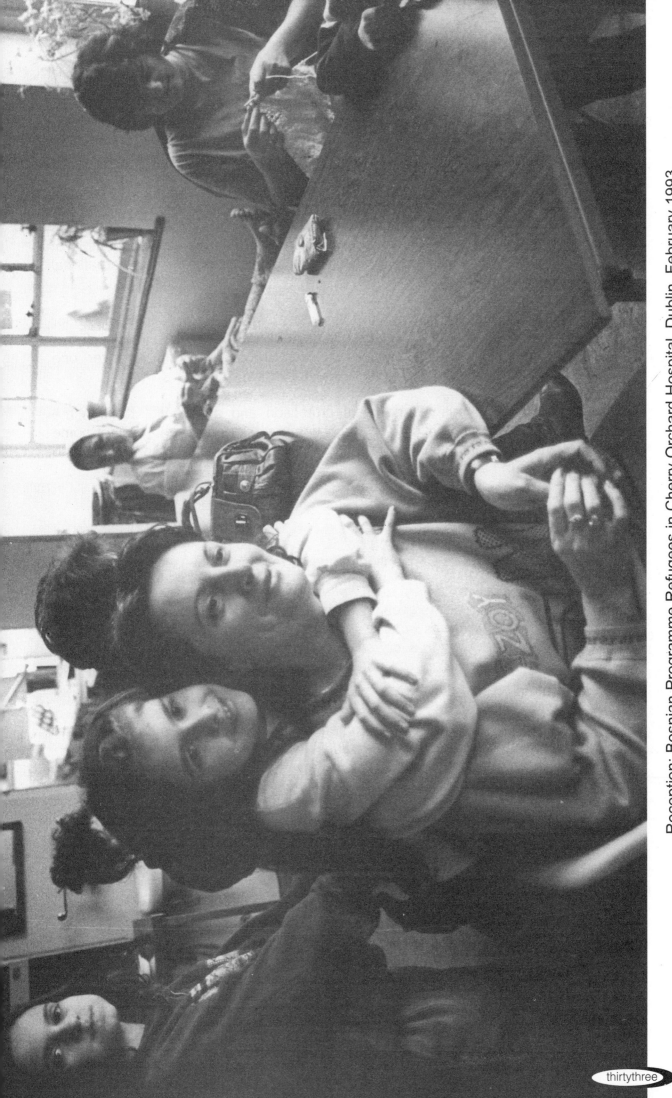

Reception: Bosnian Programme Refugees in Cherry Orchard Hospital, Dublin. February 1993
Photographer : Derek Speirs / Report

After the Second World War, the 1951 Convention was developed to cater for all refugees before 1951, and removed the historical and geographical limitations on the definitions of refugee which were in use in prior agreements. The 1951 Convention made the definition of 'refugee' universal, not tied to time or place.

The Convention and United Nations Office of the High Commissioner for Refugees (UNHCR) was established on the 1st January 1951, on a temporary basis with a mandate of three years. However, the continued need for the UNHCR led to its uninterrupted existence to date and there is no evidence that it is becoming redundant. In fact, the growing number of refugees world-wide has increased the need for a co-ordinated international response.

In 1967, the Protocol to the Refugee Convention was developed for refugees after 1951, and recognised the changing pattern of refugee movements, including those from non-European countries. Over one hundred countries have signed this Protocol.

The UNHCR has extended its protection and assistance, through the system of 'Good Offices', to large numbers of people who did not come under the 1951 Convention, including internally displaced people and victims of natural disasters.

Definitions

The 1951 Geneva Convention defines a refugee as:

> *A person who owing to a well-founded fear of being persecuted for reasons or race, religion, nationality, membership of a social group or political opinion, is outside the country of his or her nationality and is unable, or owing to such fear, unwilling to avail himself of the protection of that country; or who not having a nationality and being outside the country of his former habitual residence as a result of such events, is unable or, owing to such fear is unwilling to return to it.*

Refugee is a legal status conferred on an individual whose personal circumstances meet the criteria stipulated in the 1951 Convention. Section 2 of the Refugee Act, 1996, incorporates the 1951 Convention definition of a refugee into Irish Law. Refugee status entitles the holder to the same rights and privileges as those conferred by law on people who live in Ireland but are not Irish citizens. These rights include the rights to work, to education, to medical care and social welfare benefits, to travel in and out of the State, to practice his or her religion, to have access to the courts, and to join associations and trade unions (Refugee Act, 1996, Section 3). Like other non-national residents, refugees can apply for residence after one year, and for citizenship after three years.

Although this definition covers a variety of people and social groups who may need to seek asylum, it is not comprehensive. People may suffer persecution for reasons other than those accounted for by the definition, including women, war resisters, deserters, or people suffering from indiscriminate human rights violations because of their gender, sexuality, disability or other factors. For example, we should not forget that homosexuals and people with disabilities suffered persecution in the Nazi concentration camps.

A **Convention Refugee** is any individual who seeks refuge in a host society and is granted refugee status under the terms of the 1951 *Convention.*

A **Programme Refugee** is defined in Section 24 of the Irish Refugee Act, 1996, as:

> *a person to whom leave to enter and remain in the state for temporary protection or resettlement as part of a group of persons has been given by the Government…whether or not such a person is a refugee within the meaning of the definition of 'refugee' of section 2 (of the Refugee Act 1996)*

An **Asylum-Seeker** is any individual who has applied for refugee status under the criteria of the 1951 Convention.

> *Asylum-seeker is a temporary status conferred on the individual while their host government determines their right to full refugee status. As asylum seekers have notified the relevant authorities of their presence in the state and have lodged a claim for refugee status, they are not illegal immigrants. (Galvin, 2000)*

Individuals may be granted **Humanitarian Leave to Remain** at the discretion of the Minister for Justice. This may be granted to a person, who, for example, does not meet the requirements of the definition of a refugee under the Convention, but who the Minister decides should be allowed to remain in the State for humanitarian reasons. The Refugee Act 1996 does not stipulate the criteria used for granting an asylum seeker humanitarian leave to remain or what the individual's rights and entitlements are thereafter. (Galvin, 2000).   Byrne notes that individuals granted humanitarian leave to remain are

> *relegated to secondary legal and social status within Irish society, whereby ministerial discretion, rather than the law, will determine most of their entitlements.* (Byrne,1997: 108).

Who is not a refugee?

There is some confusion over who is, or is not, a refugee. The terms 'asylum-seeker', 'refugee', 'economic migrant' and 'illegal immigrant' have been conflated and are sometimes used interchangeably.

The UN Convention and the Irish Refugee Act (Section 2) outline who is not a refugee. This includes a person who:

◆ is receiving from organs or agencies of the UN (other than the High Commissioner) protection or assistance
◆ is recognised by the competent authorities of the country in which he or she has taken residence as having the rights and obligations which are attached to the possession of the nationality of that country

- has committed a crime against peace, a war crime, or a crime against humanity, as defined in the international instruments drawn up to make provision in respect of such crimes
- has committed a serious non-political crime outside the State prior to his or her arrival in the State, or
- has been guilty of acts contrary to the purposes and principles of the United Nations.

Refugees and economic migrants

The UNHCR Handbook on Procedures and Criteria for Determining Refugee Status defines an economic migrant as someone who:

for reasons other than those contained in the definition, voluntarily leaves his country in order to take up residence elsewhere...if he is moved exclusively by economic considerations, he is an economic migrant and not a refugee. (UNHCR website: www.unhcr.ch)

A useful way to distinguish between a refugee and a migrant is that

a migrant enjoys the protection of his or her home government; a refugee does not. (ibid).

The difference between refugees and economic migrants can sometimes be blurred. For example, where economic migrants are not assured of protection from hunger by their home government, they can be described as economic refugees. As Cullen points out, famine has become one of the major weapons of war, and those fleeing famine caused by war are effectively refugees. Cullen, (2000: 12).

The terms 'illegal immigrant' and 'asylum-seeker' are sometimes confused. In many countries, asylum seekers do not have the right to work while waiting for their application to be processed. However, many may be skilled and want to work while they are waiting and, because they receive minimal welfare payments, may need to supplement income. If they do so, they may be perceived as illegal immigrants, despite their declared asylum-seeker status.

Responsibilities under the 1951 Convention

Ratification of the Convention is not merely a statement of principle and cannot be entered into lightly. The Convention asserts not only the obligation of refugees towards the country of residence, but also the obligations of States towards refugees. States should ensure that refugees are treated at least as favourably as other aliens. Non-discrimination and a minimum standard of religious freedom should be observed. The granting of asylum itself, however, is the prerogative of the State. Technically speaking, a State may recognise a person's refugee status, yet have a right not to grant asylum to that person. However in Europe, recognition of status has come to mean the granting of asylum. (Joly, 1996: 8)

A key provision of the Convention is the prohibition of **Refoulement,** which is the expulsion of a person from the state, or the returning of a person:

in any manner whatsoever to the frontiers of territories where his life or freedom would be threatened on account of his race, religion, nationality, membership of a particular social group or political opinion.

Under the Irish Refugee Act, 1996, Section 5, the Minister for Justice, Equality and Law Reform is responsible for deciding whether particular 'territories' would threaten the life or freedom of a person.

If a State does not grant a person the right to asylum, the person may still be granted permission to stay or 'leave to remain' for humanitarian reasons. The prohibition of refoulement may be invoked for this purpose.

Other international agreements also may be invoked to justify permission to stay, for example the 1984 Convention against Torture and Other Cruel Inhuman or Degrading Treatment or Punishment, Article 3, which prevents States from returning someone to a situation where he or she could be tortured. The European Convention on Human Rights and Fundamental Freedoms also prohibits inhuman and degrading treatment (Article 3), and protects the right to live with one's family (Article 8).

These international agreements do not, however, offer guidelines to States about the treatment of people who are given leave to remain. They do not award the same quality of rights and conditions of settlement, as does the Convention. Each country decides what rights to grant those who have been given permission to stay. It has been argued by NGOs that governments have thereby assigned refugees to an alternative status in order to avoid the commitments involved in *Convention* status. (Joly, 1996: 11)

Other international agreements

Other international instruments have also been developed to respond to the changing nature of refugee movements. These include:

◆ *The Organisation of African Unity Convention Governing the Specific Aspects of Refugee Problems in Africa (1969);*
◆ *The Cartagena Declaration by the Organisation of American States (1984);*
◆ *The Manila Declaration on the Internal Protection of Refugees and Displaced Persons in Asia.*

Factors Affecting Asylum Policies

Many factors affect the development of policies for refugees and asylum seekers, and these policies need to be considered in the light of national attitudes towards the entry of all foreigners and immigrants. Joly argues:

What is at stake is nothing less than a question of sovereignty, as there seems to be universal agreement on states' exclusive authority on who can be admitted into the country and into the community of citizens. (Joly, 1996: 17)

Domestic policy

The interests of the economy and ideological and cultural issues have a bearing on asylum policies. In times of economic boom and labour shortages, reception policies tend to be more generous and relaxed than in times of recession (Joly, 1996:21). For example, under the British European Volunteer Workers (EVW) programme, between 1946 and 1949, 80,000 men and women were recruited from displaced persons' camps in Austria and Germany to work in essential industries such as mines, textiles, in hospitals and on the land. (Kay and Miles, 1992) During periods of economic recession, however, when increasing unemployment may be perceived to result from excess labour, States tend to restrict the number of refugees they are willing to accept and public attitudes may be more hostile to immigration. (Joly, 1996: 22)

Cultural and ideological issues also influence asylum policies. National identity and public reaction to asylum seekers have in the past influenced state decisions to allow asylum seekers to enter, and to determine which asylum seekers should be allowed to enter. For example, in 1945, when the Irish Government was debating whether Jews should be granted asylum in Ireland, the argument was advanced that:

because Jews do not become assimilated with the native population like other immigrants, there is a danger that any big increase in their numbers might create a social problem. (cited in Ward, 1998)

A year later, in 1946, after a request to admit 100 Jewish children from Poland, it was argued that, because of assimilation difficulties, 'they would be an irritant in the body politic'. (cited in Ward, 1998: 134)

Also when Ireland offered asylum to over 500 Hungarians in 1956, its additional criteria specified that 'they would be suitable on grounds of race and religion to ensure assimilation'. (Ward, 1998: 134)

Joly argues that:

most countries specify negative criteria defining politically or socially unacceptable people, criteria which supposedly are in conflict with national interest including State security, physical security of the nation's population and territory, economic well-being and the preservation of institutions and values. (Joly, 1996: 25)

Foreign policy

International relations and specific national foreign policy interests are also factors in the development of refugee policy. The relationship of the country of origin to the receiving country is important. For example, during the Cold War, refugees from communist regimes in Eastern Europe and Cuba were welcomed in the USA (Rystad, 1990). If a State accepts asylum-seekers from another country, it implies criticism of the regime in the country of origin; thus changing relations between States may affect willingness to accept asylum-seekers from a particular country. For example, Loescher and Scanlan (1985) suggest that the USA's refusal of asylum to large numbers of asylum seekers from Salvador and Guatemala - despite documented human rights violations in those countries - was linked to US perception of Salvador and Guatemala as allies against Cuba, Nicaragua and other communist states.

In order to process asylum applications, it is necessary to gather information about the country of origin. Embassies and official agencies in the country of origin may be reluctant to admit to human rights violations in the country they represent, and so information may be unreliable or need to be supplemented from other sources.

However, Joly argues that the increasing importance of the human rights debate has placed international obligations on States to recognise human rights. This means that States feel pressure to play their part in receiving refugees, even though they may be reluctant to invoke international condemnation about violations of human rights. (Joly, 1996: 33)

Changing Constructs of Asylum

In the post-war period, 1945 - 1970, mass migration into Europe took place because of the need for increased labour. Migration from the periphery of Europe to Western Europe occurred under 'guest worker' systems, as for example with the migration of Turks and Italians to Germany, and the migration of 'colonial workers' to former colonial powers. Because of the need for labour, many refugees sought entry to a country under the normal immigration system rather than by claiming asylum (Joly, 1996: 47). In other cases, countries specifically admitted refugees as workers, as in the previously cited case of British Government recruitment of refugees under the European Voluntary Worker (EVW) scheme. However, these migrants were tied to designated jobs, had no family reunification rights and could be deported for misconduct. (Castles and Miller, 1998: 68)

From the mid-1970s the situation in Europe began to change. Economic recession and increasing unemployment made States less receptive to immigrants. This resulted in an increased number of asylum-seekers, since those seeking asylum could no longer enter as labour migrants.

The number of asylum-seekers also increased because more people were fleeing persecution arising from war, national crises and dictatorships - for example, from Vietnam, Cambodia, Laos, Zaire, Uganda, Namibia, South Africa, Argentina and Chile. (Castles and Miller, 1998: 87)

Joly suggests a further factor in the increasing number of asylum seekers, *'cheap air travel combined with satellite communication media',* made Europe more accessible mentally and physically to those outside Europe. (Joly, 1996: 11)

The number of refugees seeking asylum in Western Europe remained fairly stable until the early 1980s. However, during the early 1990s, the map of Europe altered. When the Cold War ended, many more people from former Eastern Bloc countries moved to Western Europe, both as economic migrants and as asylum-seekers. The war in Yugoslavia also led to large

numbers of people seeking refuge in Western Europe. The number of new asylum seekers in Western European countries increased from 116,000 in 1981 to 695,000 in 1992. (OECD, 1995: 195)

In consequence of this rapid increase, Western States have tried to restrict the numbers of asylum applicants. However they must do this without infringing on humanitarian principles. Cullen (2000:12) suggests that this *'can only be achieved by bending the definition of asylum'.* The interpretation of 'persecution' has become less liberal, and Grahl-Madsen points out that:

> *there appears to be a tendency for authorities to contend that people ought to endure more in the way of hardships - political as well as economic - before they give up their homes and seek refugee status abroad.* (cited in Joly, 1996: 12)

In some countries, governments have developed the practice of excluding people who have been persecuted by so-called 'non-state agents', such as rebels or religious extremists. For example, the Federal Administrative Court in Germany ruled that people fleeing Afghanistan's Taliban rulers could not qualify for refugee status because the Taliban were not recognised as a government (Cullen, 2000:12). Such definitional shifts mean that many of the people who do not fit the exact criteria of 'refugee' are refused, and are at risk of being returned to their death or to persecution (Joly with Nettleton and Poulton, 1992).

Joly argues that, because only a small number of asylum-seekers obtain *Convention* refugee status, others are considered to be 'fraudulent'. New discourses about asylum-seekers have developed, and there is a widespread belief in Western Europe that many asylum-seekers are really economic migrants or illegal immigrants, who use claims of persecution as a means to gain entry to a country (Joly, 1996: 12). This has resulted in the notion of 'asylum-seeker' or 'refugee' being criminalised, which contravenes the spirit of the Geneva Convention. To be considered 'bogus' until they prove themselves innocent or persecuted can be an ordeal for asylum-seekers, especially when traumatised and when they do not have the language of the host country.

Recent conflicts in the former Yugoslavia highlighted many of these issues. While it may be easier to consider refugees from distant or developing countries as 'bogus', those fleeing the former Yugoslavia were Europeans and undeniably in fear of their lives. Receiving countries had to respond quickly. Prior lack of legislation in Europe to deal with refugees meant that new legislation was developed in *ad hoc* fashion, and the 'temporary protection' that emerged in Europe has been criticised both for its procedures and for its inadequate attention to social rights. (Joly, 1996:13).

European harmonisation and restriction of asylum

In response to these developments, EU member states have begun to harmonise their immigration policies, a process which has become known as the creation of 'Fortress Europe'.

The *Schengen Convention* came into force on 1 September 1993, resulting in the end of border controls and in free travel between member states. This treats refugees in the same manner as other aliens holding a residence permit from one of the contracting states; it allows them to enjoy freedom of movement within the Schengen states, providing they declare themselves to the competent authorities on arrival or within three days of entry. Asylum-seekers however are not allowed to move out of the country of application.

The *Dublin Convention,* which came into force in 1997, was the first major step to co-ordinate asylum policies in Europe. Its main aim was to establish the country responsible for asylum requests.

The most important results of these Conventions are that:

◆ each asylum application should be examined by one single state, and
◆ information should be exchanged between signatory states on matters such as national procedures, number of asylum applications, origin of asylum applicants, the country of origin, and more specific information on individual asylum-seekers.

The *Maastricht Treaty* in 1992 empowered EU Justice and Home Affairs ministers to establish a framework for a European-wide asylum policy. The first non-binding Resolutions and Conclusions included the:

◆ *Safe Third Country concept,* which allows States to refuse individuals access to their asylum procedures if the applicant could have sought protection in another 'safe' country. Asylum-seekers can seek asylum only in one EU State, and an applicant can be deported to their 'first country of application'.

◆ *Manifestly Unfounded concept,* which gives States scope to reject asylum requests on formal grounds and to limit appeal possibilities. The Irish Refugee Act specifies twelve conditions under which an application may be considered 'manifestly unfounded' (section 12). The first condition concerns an application which 'does not show on its face any grounds for the contention that the applicant is a refugee'. Other conditions apply where an applicant has not provided sufficiently detailed evidence to substantiate their claim, or where the Commissioner is satisfied that the applicant's reason for leaving or not returning to the country of nationality does not relate to a fear of persecution.

◆ *Safe Country of Origin,* which allows for accelerated procedures to process asylum applications in the case of claimants from countries in which there is generally deemed to be no serious risk of persecution.

A report commissioned by the Department of Justice, Equality and Law Reform entitled *Refugee Law Comparative Study* (1999) reviewed asylum policies in all EU states in order to ascertain what changes to the 1996 Irish Refugee Act might be necessary to align Irish policy more closely with that of our EU partners.

Ireland's Response to Refugees and Asylum-Seekers

Historically, Ireland has never had to deal with large-scale immigration, whether of refugees and asylum-seekers or labour migrants. Ward (1998) argues that this has been primarily for two reasons. The first is Ireland's geographical and political isolation in the first half of the twentieth century, which prevented it from being an accessible place for large numbers of asylum-seekers. Secondly, Ireland had its own substantial concerns as it began to establish itself as a State. It was a country of out-migration, with high levels of unemployment, and did not consider itself a country that could offer protection to victims of persecution.

However, Ireland has been affected by the dramatic political changes in Europe over the past twenty years and these changes have required that it develop strategies to deal with larger numbers of immigrants, refugees and asylum-seekers than hitherto. The resulting policies have tended to be *ad hoc* and have occasioned much debate. For example, until the introduction of a work-permit system in 2000, those who wished to enter the country, either as refugees or as labour migrants, could do so only through the asylum process. This led to delay and some confusion between refugees, economic refugees and labour migrants.

Table 1:	Chronology of Ireland's response to Aliens : 1935 – 2000
1935	**Aliens Act.** **Nationality and Citizenship Act** These 2 Acts provided the domestic legal framework for processing refugee applications until the Refugee Act in 1996
1939	**2,610 Aliens** in Ireland - 1,297 from USA, 326 from Germany, 189 from Italy,160 from France, 126 from Russia
1939-1945	588 aliens accepted – most from Germany and Austria
1946	**Aliens Order.** A hierarchy of visa applications applied : precedence was given to those from the USA, Belgium, Holland, France, Liechtenstein, Scandinavian countries.
1951	846 refugees in the State. This number fell to 450 in 1953.
1956	**Ireland signed the Convention relating to the Status of Refugees** 530 Hungarians arrived – most of whom used Ireland as a transit country and subsequently settled in North America.
1973-1974	120 Chileans arrived – most returned to Chile when democracy was restored
1979	212 Vietnamese arrived and were resettled in Ireland. Their numbers rose to 408 in 1989 under the Family Reunification programme.
1985	26 Iranian Bahái's arrived
1989	**Prohibition of Incitement to Hatred Act**
1992	178 Bosnian refugees accepted; later joined by family members and others. The Bosnian community now numbers circa 800.
1993	362 asylum applicants – until 1993, annual applicants averaged 50.
1994	The number of asylum applicants began to increase significantly.
1996	**Refugee Act**
1998	**Employment Equality Act**
1999	**Immigration Act** 1000 Kosovan Albanians accepted .
2000	**Equal Status Act** **Refugee Act 1996 (As amended) on 20 November, 2000** **Illegal Trafficking Act**

Historical overview

Table 1 above summarises milestones in Ireland's response to refugees

Ward (1998) suggests that the Irish response to refugees has developed in three phases.

The first period, from the foundation of the state until UN membership in 1956, was characterised by closure towards the plight of refugees and asylum-seekers. During the early years of the state, Ireland had to contend with its own problems arising from the War of Independence and the Civil War. Before the outbreak of the Second World War, whilst offering funding to the Vatican and the Red Cross to aid the victims of war, the State argued that, as a country of out-migration with high rates of unemployment, Ireland could not offer shelter to the displaced of Europe.

It may be argued that Ireland's closure to the plight of refugees was due not only to economic and social constraints, but also to ideological concerns. For example, in 1945, when Europe was in turmoil after the Second World War, the Department of Justice argued that up to 250 refugees could be admitted, but that the immigration of Jews to Ireland should be *'generally discouraged'* as they did not assimilate well and, a significant increase in their numbers would 'excite opposition'   (Ward, 1996:134).

In 1951, the Council of Europe, as part of intergovernmental activities to co-ordinate refugee relief in Europe, requested that all European states account for all persons who conformed to the UN Convention definition of a refugee. Ireland submitted that there were 846 such persons in the state.

Ward terms ***the second period*** of Irish response to refugees, from 1956 to the 1980s, the period of 'reluctant participation in refugee regimes'. During this period, Ireland accepted programme refugees, but did not provide for their resettlement. This period saw the arrival of Hungarian (1956), Chilean (1973-1974), Vietnamese (1979) and Iranian Bahái (1985) programme refugees. There is still little known about the number of individual asylum applications to Ireland during this period.

Acceptance of the Chilean and the Iranian Bahái refugees into the State resulted from lobbying by private citizens and groups, and to a large extent, their integration and resettlement were sponsored privately. The Chileans were sponsored by an *ad hoc* group of individuals who formed the Committee for Chilean Refugees in Ireland. The Iranian Bahái's were sponsored by the National Spiritual Assembly of the Bahái's of the Republic of Ireland. (Ward, 1996). The Hungarian and Vietnamese resettlement programmes, however, were sponsored by the State. (Ward, 1996; McGovern, 1990).

In ***the third period***, from the late 1980s to date, Ward suggests that the State began to adopt a more active response to the global plight of refugees and asylum seekers. Many more asylum-seekers were arriving in Ireland, and it became evident that there was a deficit in domestic legislation to enact the requirements and responsibilities of the 1951 Convention: Ireland was one of the few countries that did not have a legislative base to deal with applications. Ireland's changing response to refugees and asylum-seekers was also prompted by demands for change from the EU, which sought the co-ordination of member state's policies, and which resulted in the signing of the Dublin Convention and the Schengen Agreement. (Ward, 1998:45).

The response of the State to the growing number of asylum-seekers was beset with difficulties. As well as deficits in domestic legislation, resources and trained personnel, a large backlog in processing applications had developed. From 1994 the number of asylum applicants began to increase dramatically (see Table 2). It was only in 1996 after the Refugee Act that three full-time staff were employed to process asylum applications. As applicants continued to increase, staffing increased to 16 in 1997, 72 in 1998 and 144 in 1999. Many of these additional staff were retired Gardaí and civil servants. Refugee groups and human rights organisations questioned the suitability of staff, *'whose working career has been spent in a much more insular, closed Ireland to deal with the new realities of international human rights.'* (Cullen, 2000: 29). Despite the increase in staff, 10, 759 applicants were still waiting to be processed by the end of March 2001.

Table 2: Number and outcome of Asylum Applications : 1992 – March 2001

Year	No of Applicants	Granted Refugee Status	Granted Status Following Appeal
1992	39	7	1
1993	91	9	1
1994	362	34	1
1995	424	90	11
1996	1179	172	94
1997	3883	135	305
1998	4626	116	114
1999	7724	166	351
2000	10938	200 and 11 Recommendations	394
2001	2309 to end of March	84 Recommendations to end of April	

Source: Department of Justice, Equality and Law Reform

◆ *Figures on outcome of applications refer to the year in which the application was lodgedand not the year in which the decision was made*

◆ *Figures on outcome of applications do not include those who were granted Leave to Remain or those who withdrew their application*

◆ *Since November 17th 2000, the Refugee Applications Commissioner recommends Refugee Status rather than granting it.*

The majority of asylum applicants in Ireland come from Nigeria and Romania. In the first quarter of 2001, 854 (37%) Nigerians, 277 (12%) Romanians, 99 (4.3%) Moldovians, 83 (3.6%) Ukranians and 81 (3.5%) Croatians applied for asylum. There were 915 (39.6%) asylum applications from other countries. The number of asylum-seekers that Ireland receives is, however, still relatively small compared with other European countries. (Hanlon, 2000).

Table 3:   Number of Asylum applicants in selected European counties in 2000

Austria	18, 280	Norway	10, 320
Belgium	42, 690	Spain	7, 040
Denmark	10, 080	Sweden	16, 370
France	38, 590	Switzerland	17, 660
Germany	78, 760	Netherlands	43, 890
Ireland	10, 920	UK	97, 860

Source: United Nations website: www.unhcr.ch

In 1991, the Refugee Agency was established to co-ordinate the admission, reception and resettlement of Convention refugees. Its brief did not include asylum-seekers and much of its work involved policy formation.

for the first time, a denominated actor existed within the state machinery, with a budget, clear lines of authority, and interdepartmental and inter-sectoral structure and a clearly defined brief for refugees. (Ward, 1998: 46).

Consequently, when Bosnian refugees arrived in Ireland in 1992, there was a comprehensive reception and resettlement programme in place.

Recent developments in legislation and service provision

In 1996, the Department of Justice, Equality and Law reform produced new guidelines on processing asylum applicants. It was established that asylum-seekers' immediate physical needs, such as housing and health care, and other needs such as English language tuition, should be met.

In February 1999, a Refugee Legal Service was established, which gives asylum applicants the opportunity to avail of legal assistance and/or representation at all stages of the asylum process. However, only 10% of applicants avail of the service at the first stage of the process, while many more avail of it at the appeals stage. This may be one of the reasons that there is a higher level of success at appeal stage. Approximately 30% of those granted refugee status receive it at appeals stage.

In November 1999, a Central Directorate for Asylum Support Services was established under the aegis of the Department of Justice, Equality and Law Reform. It was responsible for accommodating and co-ordinating the provision of services to asylum-seekers, including the dispersal and resettlement of asylum-seekers, liaison with Local Authorities and Health Boards, and monitoring the ongoing operation of the resettlement process.

In 2000, the Directorate for Asylum Support Services was amalgamated with the Refugee Agency and is now called the Reception and Integration Agency, a statutory agency whose responsibilities include co-ordinating and implementing integration policy for all refugees and for those granted humanitarian leave to remain. They also respond to crisis situations which result in relatively large numbers of refugees arriving in Ireland within a short period of time.

The Refugee Act in 1996 provided the first piece of legislation to deal with refugees and asylum-seekers, but its full implementation was delayed; for example, The Refugee Commissioner was not appointed until December 2000. The Refugee Act was subsequently amended by the Immigration Act, 1999 and the Illegal Immigrants (Trafficking) Act, 2000, in full, on 20 November, 2000.

The Immigration Act, 1999, gives the Minister added powers, if considered necessary, to deport non-nationals, including asylum seekers, whose claims have been declared manifestly unfounded or who have not been granted refugee status through the asylum process.

The Refugee Act (as amended) provides for a new statutory system for processing asylum applications in the State, including the establishment of two new independent statutory offices: the Refugee Applications Commissioner and the Refugee Appeals Tribunal. It also provides for the establishment of a Refugee Advisory Board, which advises the Minister for Justice, Equality and Law Reform on all aspects of asylum and refugee policy.

Asylum-seekers themselves have also been active in founding refugee and asylum-seeker associations and organisations, such as ARASI (Association of Refugees and Asylum-Seekers in Ireland). These organisations play a large part in filling gaps in provision for social and other needs of asylum seekers.

Equality Legislation

Topical debates on the increase in racism in Ireland have been fuelled by the arrival of refugees and asylum-seekers. Racism and discrimination have become major areas of concern to the public and state alike. Until 1989, there was no domestic legislation to protect people who had been discriminated against because of their racial, ethnic or cultural status. The introduction of the Prohibition of Incitement to Hatred Act in 1989, was the first piece of legislation in Ireland prohibiting racism or discrimination. It is, however, little used, because it is difficult to prove that a person or body

incited hatred.

In July 1998, the National Consultative Committee on Racism and Inter-culturalism was established. The Consultative Committee is a partnership of non-governmental organisations, state agencies, social partners and Government departments. It provides a structure to develop integrated programmes and actions against racism and to advise the Government on matters relating to racism and inter-culturalism.

Recently, the Minister for Justice, Equality and Law Reform introduced two major pieces of equality legislation. The first was the Employment Equality Act of 1998, which outlaws discrimination in work related areas, including access to employment, promotion, training and work experience, on nine distinct grounds – gender, marital status, family status, sexual orientation, religion, age, disability, race, and membership of the Traveller community.

An *Equality Authority* was also established on the same day as the 1998 Act. This Authority provides support to those who are experiencing discrimination through provision of information, advice and a free legal representation service.

The second piece of equality legislation was the *Equal Status Act,* which was passed by the Oireachtas in February 2000. This complements the Employment Equality Act by giving protection against discrimination in non-workplace areas, such as education, provision of goods, services and accommodation, and disposal of property. 'Services' within the Act include entertainment and transport facilities. It also prohibits discrimination on the grounds of gender, marital status, family status, sexual orientation, religion, age, disability, race, colour, nationality, national or ethnic origin, and membership of the Traveller community.

With the enactment of the Equal Status Act 2000, Ireland can proceed to ratify the International Convention on the Elimination of All Forms of Racial Discrimination, which required the introduction of domestic legislation to ensure that the provisions of the Convention could be given full effect at domestic level. The introduction of the Equal Status Act also means that Ireland will lift its reserve on the *UN Convention on the Elimination of all Forms of Discrimination against Women.*

Conclusion

Since the 1951 Convention, the need for comprehensive legislation and policy to accommodate the growing number of asylum-seekers world-wide has become apparent. Although other European countries had developed legislation to deal with refugees and asylum-seekers, Ireland only began to co-ordinate its services and develop relevant legislation in the 1990s. Until the 1990s, Ireland did not perceive itself as a country of immigration, but in response to economic changes and its responsibilities under international agreements, Ireland has had to open its doors. Pressure to admit refugees and asylum-seekers has also come from the EU and the UN to share some of the international responsibility arising from the dramatic increase in the number of people seeking asylum globally.

Ireland's gradual acceptance of responsibilities to refugees and asylum-seekers meant that initial attempts to accommodate them were *ad hoc* and designed on a temporary basis. As it has become apparent that the number of refugees and asylu-seekers seeking asylum in the State will continue to grow, there have been many positive measures to change policies, legislation and attitudes to asylum-seekers and refugees. It remains to be seen how accepting Irish society will be of these changes and of the new role that Ireland plays as part of a global economy.

Key Readings

Joly, D (1996), *Haven or Hell? Asylum Policies and Refugees in Europe*, *London:* MacMillan Press.

Cullen, P (2000), *Refugees and Asylum-Seekers in Ireland.* Cork: Cork University Press.

Egan, S and Costello, K (1999), *Refugee Law Comparative Study.* Dublin: Faculty of Law, University College Dublin.

Ward, E (1998), 'Ireland and refugees / asylum-seekers: 1922-1996', in Lentin, R (ed), *The Expanding Nation: Towards a Multi-Ethnic Ireland. Conference Papers.* Dublin : Department of Sociology, Trinity College Dublin

CHAPTER THREE

THE EXPERIENCE OF REFUGEES AND ASYLUM-SEEKERS IN IRELAND

Introduction

As we have seen in the previous chapter, the Republic of Ireland, traditionally a country of out-migration, is increasingly becoming an in-migration destination. Simultaneously, the Irish population is becoming racially, ethnically and culturally more diverse. The emigration of large numbers of its people has been a historically dominant feature of Irish society. In-migration by non-Irish nationals, however, represents a significant change in the meaning attached to 'migration' in the Irish context. Among Ireland's current immigrant population are refugees and asylum-seekers from a host of countries, including: Romania, Bosnia, Vietnam, Cuba, Sri Lanka, Nigeria, Algeria, Angola, Somalia, Rwanda, Burundi, Sudan and the Democratic Peoples Republic of the Congo.

In this chapter, we turn to the experience of refugees and asylum-seekers when they reach Ireland.

Ireland as a refugee host society

Currently individuals who seek refuge in Ireland may be categorised into programme refugees, convention refugees and asylum-seekers. This three way distinction highlights the differential treatment accorded to individuals in relation to provisions for reception and resettlement and their legal status, rights and entitlements in Irish society.

Over the past 40 years six groups of programme refugees have arrived in Ireland at the invitation of the Irish Government and in co-operation with the United Nations High Commission for Refugees (UNHCR) (Table 1). Of these groups only significant numbers of Vietnamese, Bosnians and Kosovars have remained in Ireland. Individuals who have been granted refugee status under the 1951 United Nations Geneva Convention and asylum-seekers awaiting the outcome of their applications for refugee status arrive in Ireland through their own initiative.

In the period since 1992, the number of asylum seekers entering Ireland has increased (Table 2) but is still small in scale when compared with both global refugee movements and the number of asylum-seekers entering other European Union states. However, the increase in asylum applications over the past three years marks a significant transition as Ireland becomes firmly established as a refugee 'host society'.

Catering for Diversity: 'Tropical Shop', Dublin. June 2000
Photographer: Derek Speirs / Report

Acclimatising: Access Ireland outing to Phoenix Park, Dublin. Summer 1998
Photographer: Ann Moroney

Table 1: Number of Programme Refugees admitted to Ireland 1956-1999

Year	Place of Origin	Number (a)
1956	Hungary	530
1973-74	Chile	120
1979	Vietnam (b)	212
1985	Iran (Bahaí)	26
1992	Bosnia (c)	178
1993	Bosnia	13
1994	Bosnia	9
1995	Bosnia	80
1996	Bosnia	83
1997	Bosnia	89
1998	Bosnia	3
1999	Kosovo (d)	1032

Source: Galvin, 2000 : 200

Notes:

(a) Figures are for each 'new intake' and do not include those admitted under the family re-unification programme.

(b) 1979-1998: 382 relatives were admitted under the family re-unification programme

(c) 1993-1999: 833 relatives (276 in 1999) were admitted under the family re-unification programme.

(d) 1999: 21 relatives were admitted under the family re-unification programme.

Table 2 : Number of Asylum Applications in Ireland 1988-2000

Year	Number of asylum applicants
1988	49
1989	36
1990	60
1991	31
1992	39
1993	91
1994	362
1995	424
1996	1179
1997	3883
1998	4626
1999	7724
2000	10938

Source: Galvin, 2000: 200
Department of Justice, Equality and Law Reform

Table 3: Number of asylum applications submitted to EU Countries, by Year of Application, 1988 – 1998

Year	Number
1988	210,600
1989	288,100
1990	400,200
1991	512,700
1992	672, 500
1993	515,900
1994	309,900
1995	313,400
1996	260,000
1997	252,200
1998	297,000

Source: UNHCR Statistical Overview, 1997. http://www.unhcr.ch/statist/

When the number of asylum-seekers entering the state began to increase in 1994 (Table 3), Ireland was poorly equipped, at a legislative and policy level, for its new role as a 'refugee host society'. Though a signatory to the 1951 Geneva Convention, prior to 1996 Ireland had no legislation governing refugees and asylum-seekers and an inadequate bureaucratic machinery for dealing with them[1]. As we have seen in Chapter 2, significant development of legislation and policy has taken place in the past six years.

Procedures and Entitlements

Before we turn to current procedures and their implications for refugees and asylum-seekers, a reminder of basic definitions may be helpful.

Refugee
A person who owing to well-founded fear of being persecuted for reasons of race, religion, nationality, membership of a particular social group or political opinion is outside the country of his nationality and is unable or, owing to such fear, is unwilling to avail himself of the protection of that country; or who, not having a nationality and being outside the country of his former habitual residence as a result of such events, is unable or, owing to such fear, is unwilling to return to it. (1951 Geneva Convention)

Programme refugee
A person to whom leave to enter and remain in the state for temporary protection or resettlement as part of a group of persons has been given by the Government ... whether or not such a person is a refugee within the meaning of the definition of 'refugee' of section 2 .   (Refugee Act, 1996, Section 24)

---

[1] The 1935 Nationality and Citizenship Act, The 1935 Aliens Act, Amendments to the Aliens Act in 1946 and 1975, together with a letter from the Irish Minister for Justice (under whose remit refugees lie) to the UNHCR in 1985, setting out the procedure for refugee status and asylum, provided the legal framework for state policy until 1996 (Shipsey, 1994).

Asylum-seeker
Any individual who has applied for refugee status under the criteria stipulated in the 1951 Convention. Asylum-seeker is a temporary status conferred on individuals while the host Government determines their right to full refugee status. As asylum-seekers have notified the relevant authorities of their presence in the state and have the right to reside there while their application for refugee status is being assessed, they cannot be categorised as illegal immigrants.

Individuals granted humanitarian leave to remain :
Leave to remain in the state is granted at the discretion of the Minister for Justice, Equality and Law Reform. It may be accorded to a person who does not fully meet the requirements of the definition of the 1951 Convention, but who the Minister decides should be allowed to remain in the state on humanitarian grounds. (Faughnan, 1999:9)

Programme Refugees

From the time of their arrival, programme refugees have the same rights and entitlements as Irish citizens in relation to social welfare payments, housing, education, training and employment. After three years of residence in Ireland they are entitled to apply for Irish citizenship (O'Regan, 1998). Additionally, they are entitled to avail of family re-unification, through which close family members who remained in their country of origin or a third country are allowed to join them in Ireland.

The Refugee Agency[2], established in 1991 under the auspices of the Department of Foreign Affairs, was the statutory body with responsibility for programme refugees. The role of the agency was twofold: the reception and resettlement of refugees; and the establishment of services/structures and polices in relation to refugee resettlement.

Refugee reception essentially involves the provision of basic services, such as medical care and housing, at the time of arrival.

Refugee resettlement, on the other hand, refers to a broad range of activities whose ultimate aim is the integration of refugees into their host society. Resettlement includes the family reunification process; the establishment of specialist services to meet the specific needs of refugees, such as language training and psychological services; the establishment of bridging services, such as pre-vocational training to enable refugees to access mainstream services; and the adaptation of mainstream services and provisions to incorporate the needs of refugees.

Convention Refugees and Asylum-Seekers

On arrival in Ireland, asylum-seekers register with the relevant Government Department, namely the asylum division of the Department of Justice,

---

[2] In 2000, The Refugee Agency was amalgamated with the Directorate for Asylum Support Services and is now called The Reception and Integration Agency.

Equality and Law Reform. Initially, the individual is given appropriate information and an application form, where possible in his or her own language. Asylum-seekers have one week in which to complete and lodge their application form, which then constitutes their official application for refugee status. Thereafter, asylum-seekers are interviewed in relation to their application. There is no set timeframe within which interviews take place. A general lack of resources, including a shortage of staff and a backlog of applications, means that individuals frequently wait for long periods, in some instances two to three years, before their interviews take place.

Under the accelerated 'fast-track' procedures introduced in 1999, an interview may be scheduled at the initial application stage, when the claim for refugee status is judged to be either manifestly unfounded or a substantial claim. Individuals can make submissions in relation to their application during the interim period between lodging the application and their interview, and up to five days after the interview.

Where a claim for refugee status is found to be manifestly unfounded, the individual is given all the papers from their case and has seven days to lodge information stipulating why he or she should be given a more substantive hearing in the form of an appeal. An individual has two weeks in which to appeal against an unfavourable decision. Appeals are considered by the Refugee Appeal Board (Section 15 (1) of the Refugee Act, 1996) and take place between two weeks and one month after notification of the initial refusal. Unlike the initial application and interview, the appeals process is an adversarial one. Thus an individual may be granted refugee status on the basis of their original application, or after the appeals process. Both in relation to their initial application, and where necessary their appeal, asylum-seekers are entitled to avail of free legal aid.

From Asylum-Seeker to Convention Refugee

Once granted refugee status, individuals make the transition to being legally accepted as permanent members of Irish society. Individuals are informed by the Department of Justice that their rights in this State now entitle them to:

◆ Reside in the state
◆ Seek and enter employment
◆ Carry on any business, trade or profession
◆ Access to education and training in the like manner and to the like extent in all respects as an Irish citizen
◆ The same medical care and services as those to which an Irish citizen is entitled
◆ The same social welfare benefits as those to which an Irish citizen is entitled
◆ The same rights of travel in or from the State as those to which Irish citizens are entitled
◆ The same freedom to practice their religion and the same freedom as regards the religious education of their children as an Irish citizen
◆ The same access to the courts in the like manner and to the like extent

in all respects as an Irish citizen
◆ Apply to the Minister (for Justice, Equality and Law Reform) for permission to be granted to a member of their family to enter and to reside in the State, under the provision for family re-unification

In essence Convention refugees have the same rights and entitlements as Programme refugees including the right to apply for Irish citizenship.

Reception and Resettlement

Procedural and policy developments

Currently Ireland does not operate a system of detention centres in relation to asylum-seekers. Individuals are thus interacting with mainstream society from the time of arrival. The Government Directive, 1999, on the employment of asylum-seekers and the introduction of a dispersal policy in 2000 represent two significant changes in the Government's asylum policy.

The *Refugee Act,* 1996 stipulates that, in the period between arrival and acquiring refugee status, asylum-seekers are prohibited from taking up paid employment. It is suggested by the Irish Government that to allow asylum-seekers to work would create a sense of permanence for individuals whose applications for refugee status might eventually be refused. As a result, and irrespective of their educational background or skills, *asylum-seekers 'are entirely dependent on state subvention for their housing and income needs'* (O'Sullivan, 1997: 5). However, a Government directive in July 1999 stipulated that all asylum-seekers who had been resident in the state for one year on July 29th 1999 were entitled to apply for work permits and to take-up employment while awaiting the outcome of their application for refugee status. Effectively, this directive meant that all asylum-seekers who had arrived in Ireland prior to July 29th 1998 were no longer legally prohibited from seeking employment.

In December 1999, the Government adopted a *dispersal policy* in relation to new arrivals. The dispersal policy was accompanied by the introduction of: reception centres in which asylum-seekers would be housed; and *'direct provision'* as the system through which the basic needs of asylum-seekers would be met. The dispersal policy was largely a response to an accommodation crisis in Dublin (in relation to asylum-seekers) in December 1999. However, both the introduction of reception centres and direct provison can be viewed as restrictive policy measures, whose aim is to discourage individuals from applying for refugee status. Additionally, it can be argued that the Government has overemphasised the manner in which the state welfare system acts as a pull factor, thereby attracting larger numbers of asylum-seekers (Galvin, 2000). In this context, a direct provision system can be seen as a way to discourage asylum applicants. To date, the system of 'direct provision' has been applied only to those within the dispersal programme.

The changes which have ocurred in refugee policy thus give rise to a situation wherein 'date of arrival in Ireland' determines the resources

available to asylum-seekers to meet their basic needs.

The dispersal programme and direct provision system were introduced in April 2000. Asylum-seekers who arrived prior to April 2000 are entitled to many of the social welfare benefits available to Irish citizens, but are not entitled to benefits over and above those available to Irish nationals. They can claim a weekly Supplementary Welfare Allowance (SWA), a rent supplement, children's allowance, a clothing allowance on arrival, and a fuel allowance during the winter months. As in the case of all recipients of the SWA, they are entitled to a medical card and thus free health care. The children of asylum-seekers are allowed to attend school. At the time of arrival, pre-April 2000 asylum-seekers were classified as homeless and provided with temporary, emergency accommodation, either in designated hostels or in guesthouses (B & Bs). Thereafter, they rent flats and houses within the private rental sector.

Asylum-seekers experience considerable difficulty acquiring such accommodation. At the outset, individuals are unfamiliar with the layout of the city together with the bus and train routes. Asylum-seekers who are not proficient in English cannot access sources of relevant information on accommodation, such as the evening newspaper. Additionally, landlords may discriminate against those with a rent allowance or because they are foreign nationals. Finally, and in particular in the Dublin area, there is a shortage of affordable rental accommodation. As a result of the difficulties encountered in relation to rented accommodation, asylum-seekers frequently remain in emergency accommodation for long periods of time. The use of such accommodation is problematic at a number of levels. Emergency accommodation is frequently overcrowded, with the subsequent lack of privacy which this entails for individuals and family units. The temporary nature of such accommodation enhances the insecurity generally felt by asylum-seekers. Guesthouses may require individuals to vacate the premises during daytime. While such arrangements are problematic for all asylum-seekers, they are particularly so for women with young children. Where emergency accommodation does not include meals, individuals spend a disproportionate amount of their SWA on food in restaurants. Where asylum-seekers move from one emergency accommodation to another, their children's education is disrupted, with the additional trauma which this implies.

Under the system of 'direct provision,' asylum-seekers are provided with meals and accommodation together with a financial allowance ('comfort money') of £15 per week for an adult and £7.50 per week for a child. Effectively 'direct provision' places asylum-seekers outside the normal state welfare system, though they continue to have access to the state's healthcare services and the children of asylum-seekers continue to attend school.

In general, the development of asylum policy has been reactive in nature. The asylum issue has been portrayed as temporary and as an administrative and legal problem. As a consequence, policies and procedures have developed at a slow pace and in an uneven manner. At a structural level, advances have been made through the establishment of The Refugee Appeal Board, the provision of free legal aid, the centralisation of all relevant services to which new arrivals require access, and the provision of interpretation facilities. At the same time, the administrative machinery for processing asylum claims has not been adequately expanded. This, together with an increase in new arrivals in the period since September 1999, has meant that a considerable backlog of cases remains a constant feature of the asylum process in Ireland. To many asylum-seekers, their cases are processed in what appears to be a slow and inconsistent manner.

In relation to policy and procedures, the period since 1998 has seen a number of significant developments, namely: the establishment of an independent appeals board; relevant services to which new arrivals require access in one building – 'the one stop shop'. Additionally, the Department of Justice, Equality and Law Reform now seeks to ensure that female asylum applicants are interviewed by women officers.

Irish Society's Response to Refugees and Asylum-Seekers

The arrival of an increasing number of refugees and asylum-seekers has generated significant debate at all levels of Irish society. The response of the Irish population is ambiguous, complex and varied. Prior to the introduction of the dispersal programme, the majority of refugees and asylum-seekers were concentrated in Dublin. Consequently, the vast majority of the Irish population had no contact with them. Even within Dublin, there is a spatial concentration of refugees, which is largely determined by the availability of affordable housing. As a result, some of the most vulnerable areas of the city are now home to a disproportionate number of refugees and asylum-seekers. The complex response to the dispersal programme has shown that local communities are apprehensive, ambivalent, fearful and, in some cases, hostile to asylum-seekers.

Government delay in sponsoring a public information campaign has meant that large sectors of the population remain unfamiliar with the causes of refugee movements. At the same time, the degree and nature of social interaction between the Irish population and asylum-seekers and refugees is largely circumscribed by the rules governing asylum. For those who arrived prior to April 2000, the initial point of contact and thus of social interaction was frequently a local social welfare office. The context of social interaction was thus within the confines of access to state resources. Negative press coverage, an ambiguous response on the part of Government, together with the context of social interaction, have worked together to create 'resource based' tension and animosity. The resulting stereotyping of asylum-seekers as 'sponging off the welfare state' ,and the emergence of myths surrounding the level of state benefits for refugees and asylum-seekers, reinforces those same tensions. By contrast, the dispersal programme has introduced refugees and asylum-seekers to a broad range of communities in Irish society. However, the system of direct provision has the potential to severely curtail interaction between asylum-seekers and the host population.

The Refugee Experience

The waiting period

For asylum-seekers, the prolonged and indefinite periods of time taken to assess applications for refugee status are marked by:

◆ fear and uncertainty
◆ frustration and distress
◆ a heightened sense of insecurity
◆ long periods of separation from family members, for without refugee status family reunification cannot be availed of
◆ a loss of social and economic status associated with dependence on the state welfare system
◆ adjustment to the host society
◆ barriers to social interaction and integration.

Dependence on social welfare payments or direct provision means that 'asylum' represents:
◆ the inability to work, travel and engage in broad based 'normal' social interaction with the wider society.

When asylum-seekers arrive alone and family members have been left in the country of origin, this same time period involves a long separation from and constant worry about the safety of loved ones. This is particularly traumatic when:

◆ the whereabouts of loved ones becomes unclear
◆ a spouse or children cannot be located or contacted
◆ there is an upsurge in conflict in the home country
◆ loved ones die, are imprisoned or murdered
◆ the lack of available news from home adds to the uncertainty, causing feelings of loneliness, isolation and despair.

Among others, Harrell-Bond (1986), Waldron (1988) and Marx (1990) have noted the difficulties associated with the use of the term refugee. In particular the terms 'asylum-seeker' and 'refugee' portray an homogeneous category and thus fail to acknowledge the degree of diversity found therein. Any population of asylum-seekers/refugees consists of men, women and children, family units and individuals of diverse ages, socio-economic and cultural backgrounds. Additionally, there is a considerable degree of diversity in past experiences, in the causes of flight and in subsequent experiences of exile. In reality, individual asylum-seekers may have little in common other than their claim to the legal status of refugee.

Al-Rasheed (1991) and others have noted that in exile there is a reconstruction of the meaning of asylum and exile. When the label refugee takes on a negative meaning in the context of the host society, and the right to refuge is constantly questioned, refugee status is devalued. As a consequence individuals experience a crisis of meaning in relation to refugee status as they take on board the negative perceptions of their host society.

In exile, the status of refugee becomes a hindrance rather than a resource in the resettlement process. Individuals begin to deny their status as asylum-seekers and refugees when the experience of exile fails to live up to expectations; when the status itself is viewed as a barrier to interacting with the host society; and when there is genuine fear for their own safety. Such denial creates, for the individual, public and private sphere within their lives that are not easily reconciled and that have repercussions for individual self-esteem and identity. (Galvin, 2000:207)

Asylum seekers respond at different levels and in different ways to the period of prolonged waiting for a determination of their cases. For many asylum-seekers a state benefit system is new, as they come from societies where no such benefits exist. Over time, asylum-seekers and refugees become conscious of and sensitive to hostility toward them as the recipients of state benefits. In seeking accommodation, individuals become conscious of the limitations of the 'rent supplement' to which they are entitled and aware of the many Irish landlords who do not want to accept it. For those who in their home countries were employed, skilled, and middle class, dependence on state welfare is perceived as undignified and represents a loss of social status. Frustration results when asylum-seekers find that their prolonged temporary status and dependence on social welfare act as barriers to resettlement and integration into the host society. Exile also involves the re-definition of social roles. For the male asylum-seeker, whose previous role incorporated that of family head, long periods of unemployment can and do translate into the loss of his role as family breadwinner, with a resulting loss of dignity and status within the family unit and the wider community.

Zetter (1991) notes that, within the confines of the host society, the label refugee can have a narrow and materialist meaning. At the same time, the constant questioning of 'the individual's right to refuge' gives rise to a perception that asylum-seekers are essentially seeking to deceive the system (Fuglerud, 1997). The loss of the breadwinner role, and the perceived decrease in social status, are all the more difficult when the host society emphasises social welfare payments as pull factors in refugee movements, to the exclusion of push factors, such as war and human rights abuses.

Constructing a new life

Hirschon (1989) notes that:

refugees try to establish familiar patterns and maintain continuity with their past in an attempt to overcome personal alienation and social disintegration.

The experience of exile is shaped by factors which determine the individual's position in the host society. In the Irish case, the most significant factors of this kind are policies which result in 'restrictive inclusion' at different levels of the society, and the subsequent manner in which the status of asylum-seeker and refugee is seen as demeaning and without dignity.

Asylum-seekers in Ireland are active participants in constructing a life for themselves within the confines of the limited resources available to them.

They use the public library system for access to newspapers and other reading material, take language classes and other skills course aimed at enhancing existing skills or acquiring new ones. As asylum-seekers are not entitled to access the specialist services available to refugees, they are dependent on their limited financial resources to undertake courses and training programmes. The direct provision policy seriously undermines the ability of asylum-seekers to access such training. Limited or no access to training impedes the resettlement process and creates barriers to integration in the long term.

Many asylum-seekers engage in voluntary work with a host of voluntary bodies as a means of becoming familiar with Irish society and in an attempt to re-establish the dignity which is associated with work. So too, for many asylum-seekers, periods of voluntary work constitute a break in an otherwise monotonous and boring existence which is associated with being unemployed. At the same time, families and individuals begin to set up home, while others get married and begin a family life.

In dealing with the limitations of their status and the uncertainty surrounding their position, asylum-seekers in Ireland demonstrate a remarkable degree of resourcefulness. As a result, they cannot be viewed as helpless individuals, whose lives are torn apart as a result of forced migration, but as active participants in reconstructing their lives.

Perceptions of Ireland as a host society

Prior to arrival, many asylum-seekers are knowledgeable about our history and the colonial past, which we share with many of the countries from which they come. Equally, they are conscious of Ireland's struggle to develop, the unexpected arrival of an increasing number of refugees, and the confusion which this has generated. After their arrival, asylum-seekers learn about Irish society through radio and television and from their interaction with a variety of individuals and social institutions. The general lack of knowledge about refugee movements and the plight of refugees is one of the most salient issues to emerge in their perceptions of Irish society. That Irish people do not understand what it means to be a refugee is a phenomenon which many find difficult to understand, and particularly frustrating given our own history of emigration.

Asylum seekers also become knowledgeable about the traits and characteristics of Irish society. In particular, they note the attention paid to and the emphasis on 'Irish hospitality'. As residents in our midst, they begin to observe and critically question the nature of that hospitality and of other aspects of our society. Though asylum seekers appreciate the efforts Ireland is making to give them a place of safety, this does not mean that as participants they are uncritical of aspects of the asylum process or of some of the traits and characteristics of Irish society

Given the insecurity surrounding the asylum process, it is not surprising that individuals are sensitive to the manner in which they are treated by officials from the Department of Justice, Equality and Law Reform and other state institutions with which they come into contact. They note the manner in which people speak to them, the difficulty of communicating in English, and the frustration bordering on anger when people clearly do not understand their situation. Individuals recount a host of positive and negative experiences, which together constitute the experience of exile in Ireland.

Once granted refugee status, individuals find that there are very few structures in place to enable them to make the transition to being full members of Irish society. As a result, there is yet another period of uncertainty and a new set of barriers to surmount in the resettlement process. Qualifications are not always easily or readily transferable, and inadequate provision of support services leaves many refugees unable to access mainstream services and a broader range of societal resources. Both at the initial asylum stage and later as refugees, individuals have needs over and above those of Irish nationals. As a consequence, specialist services are required to meet those needs. This applies in particular to language, training and employment. It must also be noted, however, that a dependency culture should not be cultivated. Recognition of the special needs of asylum-seekers and refugees has to be balanced with the need to recognise that, as individuals, they are capable of establishing themselves in Irish society given the opportunity to do so.

Women as refugees and asylum–seekers

Women asylum-seekers and refugees are in a particularly vulnerable position. At the legislative and policy level, the complex range of issues surrounding gender based persecution, together with the specific needs of refugee women, are frequently invisible. The 1951 Geneva Convention was formulated in an era when there was little recognition of the specific forms of persecution experienced by women (Bloch, Galvin and Harrell-Bond, 2000). As the 1951 Convention remains unchanged, Bissland and Lawand (1997) note that international law does not afford women the same protection as their male counterparts. Equally, when national legislation premised upon the 1951 Convention fails to explicitly recognise gender-based persecution and its causes, women do not have equal access to or protection within the asylum process. So too, women do not always relate their experiences of persecution to the criteria stipulated in the 1951 Convention. For cultural reasons, a woman may not wish to be the principal asylum applicant, even when she has a stronger case than her male counterpart. Finally, background country reports are frequently silent on the forms of persecution suffered by women.

Though refugee legislation and policy measures may lack a gender dimension, forms of persecution do not. Men and women may experience similar forms of persecution, but there is a growing recognition of forms of persecution unique to women (UNHCR, 1990).

Due to their role and status in society generally, and more specifically within family and kinship systems, women may in fact be exposed to a wider range of human rights abuses than their male counterparts. (Bloch, Galvin & Harrel-Bond, 2000: 2)

Gender based persecution may take the form of sexual violence, as in the

case when rape is used as a weapon of war. Bates (1998) notes that rape as a war crime was recognised for the first time in 1998, in relation to the war in the former Yugoslavia. Women may also suffer persecution as a result of transgressing social norms, such as dress codes, while ritual practices, such as female circumcision, give rise to human rights concerns of specific relevance to women.

Quite apart from their own political activities, women may also be persecuted as a result of the political activities of male relatives. In this respect, and in relation to Chilean refugees, Eastmond (1993: 42) notes,

while the political drama of Chile had certainly also shaped the fates of women refugees, they identified less as political actors, and their part in the struggle was seen rather as complementary.

The sources of female persecution are therefore complex and varied, and frequently not recognised in refugee law. Bissland and Lawand (1997) note that, in EU countries, very few asylum applications are made solely on the basis of gender-based persecution, and that a far smaller number of women than men are principal asylum applicants.

At the policy and legislative level, there is much variation between countries in the manner of dealing with the gender dimension of the refugee process. While Australia and Canada have introduced gender guidelines, Denmark and Germany are developing such guidelines (Ellegaard, 1997). In Ireland, the Refugee Act, 1996, recognises gender-based persecution as grounds for an asylum application and, in so doing, recognises forms of persecution unique to women.

In Belgium, women do not necessarily interview asylum-seekers, as is the case in France, Germany, Norway and Switzerland (Bissland and Lawand, 1997). In Ireland, the Government has recently sought to ensure that women officers interview women applicants.

In Spain, women are automatically included in the asylum application of their spouse or other male relative, unless they state that they wish to make an independent claim. In England, women may choose to make an independent claim, while in Ireland each individual's claim is considered separately.

The barriers to women's full access to the asylum process are legal, social and cultural in nature. Forms of persecution experienced by women may not be catered for within the confines of international or national legal instruments. While cultural norms which dictate gender relations may preclude women from recounting their experiences in the presence of male relatives, Crawley (1997) notes that cultural norms may preclude women from taking the role of principal applicant. This applies even in cases where women have a more substantial case for refugee status than that of their male relatives.

As is the case with all those in exile, women find their role and status redefined within the cultural context of the host society. Role redefinition and a loss of status may result when women are unable to fulfil past roles.

Exile removes from women the support structure of social networks based on family and friends. This can be a particularly difficult loss for women who are denied help with childcare, and as a result find themselves isolated in their host society. Religious ideology, socio-cultural norms, and childcare responsibilities contribute to the isolation experienced by women in exile, and limit their interaction with the host society.

In exile, men frequently continue their political and community activities and, in so doing, maintain a link with their past, while also reestablishing their role and status within the community. A similar range of activities is frequently not available to women. Factors which give rise to their isolation also impact upon women's integration into the host society. Women's access to language classes and other forms of training may be severely curtailed, due to childcare responsibilities and to practices such as female seclusion. Lack of language skills and socio-cultural factors can thus combine to exclude women from social and economic participation in the host society.

There is, then, a clear need for :
◆ explicit legal recognition of gender based persecution
◆ asylum determination procedures sensitive to women's needs and experiences
◆ training programmes which accommodate the role, status and responsibilities of women.
Without such developments, women will remain marginalised and excluded from the asylum process and unable to participate effectively in resettlement programmes.

As many women are the dependants of male applicants, as opposed to principal asylum applicants, they face uncertainty about their position should they divorce, or not wish to accompany their husbands who decide to return home.

The host society confronts women with many new challenges. Their role within the home and the lack of childcare facilities make it more difficult for women to attend language classes or skills training. Yet they have to interact with schools which their children attend, hospitals when they give birth or have a sick child, and with many other social institutions. All too often, language difficulties or their cultural position leave women unable to fulfil these roles. In these circumstances, such roles are often assumed by men or older children, and women lose their status both within the family unit and their wider community.

The small number of women who are principal asylum applicants means that this is a lonely position for women. All too often, the type of political activities on which asylum applications are based are viewed as within the male public domain. Women do not find ready acceptance of their claims, either within their own communities or within the wider host society.

Asylum-Seekers' Support Networks

It should not be assumed that asylum seekers and refugees are a homogeneous group and necessarily mutually supportive. Individuals bring

their cultural background and past experiences with them into exile. In particular, they bring into exile their experiences of other groups from their own society. As a result, many refugees do not associate with members of, or ethnic groups from within, their own society, while in exile. Indeed the divisions brought from home may be so great, that they are unable to interact at all with others from their country of origin. So too, fear of their own governments can leave asylum seekers hesitant about the desirable degree of interaction with those from home.

Many, however, establish a primary network of friends from within the refugee community, which acts as a support structure especially for providing information. Additionally, asylum-seekers make friends within Irish society and, in so doing, benefit from the support structures provided by secondary networks. It is those who remain isolated from primary and secondary social networks who are in fact the most vulnerable asylum-seekers and refugees.

Conclusion

The asylum process is complex both for individual applicants and for their host society. The diversity of asylum seekers and refugees is replicated at all levels of the refugee experience and in the intersection between asylum-seekers and host society. Portrayal of the refugee experience as homogeneous at any level serves to ignore and obscure a host of factors, which are essential components of refuge, exile, reception, and resettlement of refugees. Ireland is now an established host to refugees and asylum-seekers. A successful reception and resettlement process demands attention to the complexity of the refugee world.

Key readings

Bloch, A, Galvin, T and Harrel-Bond, B (2000) 'Refugee Women, Children and Families in Europe'. *International Migration Review*, 38.2.

Byrne, R (1997), 'On the Sliding Scales of Justice: the status of Asylum-Seekers and Refugees in Ireland' in Byrne, R. and Duncan, W. (eds) *Developments in Discrimination Law in Ireland and Europe*. Dublin: Irish Centre for European Law, Trinity College Dublin

Eastmond, M. (1993), 'Life: Chilean refugee women and the dilemmas of exile' in Buijs, G. (ed.) *Migrant Women: Crossing Boundaries and Changing Identities*. Oxford: Berg.

Fuglerud, O (1997), 'Ambivalent Incorporation: Norwegian Policy towards Tamil Asylum-seekers from Sri Lanka,' *Journal of Refugee Studies*, 10.4.

Galvin, T (2000), 'Refugee Status in Exile: The Case of African Asylum-seekers in Ireland' in MacLachlan, M and O' Connell, M. *Cultivating Pluralism*. Dublin: Oaktree Press.

Harrell-Bond (B) 1986 *Imposing Aid*. Oxford: Oxford University Press.

Marx, E (1990), 'The Social World of Refugees: A Conceptual Framework,'

Journal of Refugee Studies, 3.3.

Refugee Act (1996), Dublin: Government Publications.

Zetter, R (1988), 'Refugees and Refugee Studies: a Label and an Agenda,' *Journal of Refugee Studies,* 1.1 : 1-6

Zetter, R (1991), 'Labelling Refugees: Forming and Transforming a Bureaucratic Identity' *Journal of Refugee Studies,* 4.1.

Scenarios for Discussion

Scenario 1   Leaving your country of origin

Imagine your departure. Explore the practical and emotional issues involved.

◆ Why? What has happened to make you leave?
◆ How?
◆ When?
◆ Who, if anyone is leaving with you?
◆ Whom are you leaving behind?
◆ What money, papers and resources will you need?
◆ What do you decide to take with you?
◆ What do you decide to leave behind?
◆ Whom do you tell about your departure?
◆ What do you tell them?
◆ How do you feel about leaving your family; friends; neighbours; community; workplace; church?
◆ Will you see them again?
◆ Do you know where you are going? What will it be like?

Scenario 2. Arrival

Imagine your arrival in Ireland? Through a port / airport or other? Alone? With Others?

◆ How do you feel?
◆ First impressions?
◆ Do you know where you are?
◆ With whom do you speak?
◆ How do they respond?
◆ Do you speak their language?
◆ What do the people look like?
◆ Are they friendly? Curious? Hostile? Aggressive?
◆ Where do you go?
◆ How do you ask for refugee status?
◆ How do you find accommodation?
◆ Where do you find information about services?

Scenario 3: Accommodation .

It is reported that many asylum seekers have had to live in substandard conditions:Hostels and Bed and Breakfast accommodation, that are sometimes very crowded, with poor facilities, inadequate hot water or heating; that require residents to leave for long periods each day, or to return early in the evening or risk losing their place. When residents complain, they may be asked "What do you expect?"

Imagine yourself in that situation and answer the following questions:
◆ What sort of conditions / facilities would you expect as normal?
◆ What would be your "bottom line" ?
◆ Describe your average day?
◆ What sort of difficulties would you encounter?
◆ How would you seek to resolve them?

Scenario 4: Asylum Application

You have now made an application for asylum and are waiting to be interviewed?

◆ What is it like to be waiting for an outcome?
◆ What concerns do you have?

Scenario 5: Living Life as an Asylum-Seeker

You cannot work currently. There is little to do and you cannot officially register for language classes. Even if you could, you would have difficulty arranging child care for your two young children while you attend?

◆ What does it feel like to be an asylum seeker?
◆ Describe your average day?

Scenario 6: Health

You are living in poor accommodation which is damp and inadequately heated. You are worried about your health, and would like to get a full medical check-up.

◆ What concerns do you have in this situation?

Scenario 7: Antenatal Care

You are visibly pregnant and attending the local hospital for antenatal care.

◆ How are you treated?
◆ How do you feel about being examined by a male doctor?
◆ Do hospital staff make any assumptions about your pregnancy?
◆ Or about your health status?

All pregnant women are now routinely screened for HIV infection.

◆ How do you react?   Do you object?
◆ Can you understand what the doctors and nurses say about informed consent?

Scenario 8: Expecting a Baby

Your baby is due in 2 months times. Your partner is not here with you.

◆ Can your friend / sister / contact worker be present at the birth?
◆ Will your accommodation arrangements be affected by having a small baby?
◆ If you have other children, who will care for them while you are in hospital giving birth?
◆ What will it be like for you having this baby in Ireland?

Scenario 9 : Schools

Your children are attending local schools. The teachers and principal are very supportive.

◆ Are you able to help with their homework and assignments?
◆ How do you feel about your children meeting new friends?
◆ Will their parents accept your children as their children's friends?
◆ How do you feel about your children being exposed to different customs?

Scenario 10 : Settling

You have been granted Refugee Status. At last, you and your partner have jobs and a home. Your children are settled in school, but are fast becoming Irish teenagers. Your elderly father joined you recently, under the family reunification programme.

◆ What are your hopes and concerns?
◆ How do you see the future for your family?

CHAPTER FOUR :
SERVICES AND SERVICE PROVIDERS

Introduction

An asylum-seeker is an ordinary person in an extraordinary situation

We turn now to the provision of services for Refugees and Asylum-Seekers and review some of the challenges facing service providers. The experiences of some service providers are included.

Refugees and asylum-seekers come from many different countries, have diverse reasons for flight, are of all ages, family status and social backgrounds, and have diverse needs. Because of this heterogeneity, the services they may require range from statutory and professional services through to community-based and self help groups. Moreover, because the asylum-seeking process is often lengthy, needed services range from those required at the point of arrival through to those relevant to settlement in the longer term. As a result, refugees and asylum-seekers need and make contact with both specific, dedicated services and services for the general population, and these services can be further subdivided into those provided by the state and by voluntary, non-governmental organisations.

The matrix below summarises this four-fold distinction between services.

Statutory: Specific Services	**Statutory : General services**
Reception and Integration Agency: determining status; appeals; health; accommodation; language support; counselling; resettlement	Gardai; health; social services; housing; social welfare; education; training
NGO : Specific Services	**NGO : General Services**
Refugee Council and other groups; language support; social support; housing; community development; policy groups	family support; counselling; housing advice; community services

Moran (1999) points out that the development of Irish social policy for refugees has been recent, ad hoc and reactive, changing rapidly, and not always in step with the development of general social policy. Consequently, the challenges facing service providers in each of the four sectors are considerable. Those in general services have to adapt their practices and procedures to people with new needs and different expectations, often without necessary training, resources or co-ordination. Those in specialist services rapidly develop expertise and understanding of the concerns of refugees and asylum-seekers, but have to contend with problems of funding, awareness, public resistance, and the risk of marginalisation.

Updating Skills: FAS Training Centre, Baldoyle, Dublin. May 1998
Photographer: Derek Speirs / Report

seventyone

New Dubliners: Children of Access Ireland Trainees. Dublin, 1998
Photographer: Ann Moroney

Challenges Facing Service Providers

Language

Developing fluency in the language of the host country is a hurdle for many migrants. Without the language, it is difficult to communicate needs, obtain services, access education or work, or even participate in the wider community.

It takes huge courage to buy even a stamp in the shop .... you can lose confidence and .... self esteem so much, when (you) have to think about how ... to express (yourself) all of the time. It's like a barrier and that is just so frustrating.

English is essential to access work, health services, training, official bodies, emergency services.... One woman was experiencing a lot of racism. People were throwing stones at her door and at her kids while they were playing in the garden. A friend was mugged on her doorstep and she was called names every time she went out the door. She wanted to approach the police on a few occasions, but didn't have the language to explain herself properly. Finally she did, but she didn't have the language and they didn't seem to have the time to try to understand her problem. It is the worst position to be alienated from the emergency services. You need access to the people who are there to protect you. (Language Support Worker)

Language Training

Language training is provided for those with refugee status, often in existing language schools. The Refugee Language and Support Unit supplements this provision through three programmes: a) community outreach programmes; b) vocational and language training courses for those with refugee status who are seeking work; c) English language classes for Programme Refugees.

Since linguistic proficiency is needed for so many aspects of life in a new country, language teachers need to respond creatively to the needs of refugees and to support language development in the areas of most significance to them.

We try to encourage them to do lots of stuff at home as well.. one of the things that is very helpful is the Teletext, where you can watch a TV programme and the text comes up...We would encourage them to listen to radio stations.........we would bring the newspapers in and maybe talk about something that is in them. They use a lot of different ways of learning. (Language Support Worker)

Even though we base the course on modules, we are very much into autonomous learning and a flexible approach, where we do a lot of group work, or working on their own, or in pairs, on a particular topic or skill that they are interested in.... We say that it is their course, not our course. (Vocational Support worker)

The success of specialised language and vocational modules is reflected in the enthusiasm with which providers talk of the impact of services on their users.

Some women say that they are a lot more independent. One woman .. wrote a very good letter to the Refugee Agency about why her mother should come (under the family reunification scheme). Another woman felt great about being able to go to the doctor on her own without her teenage son being there, and another woman just felt so good about being able to go to the Department of Justice to get her new identity card....... I get tremendous satisfaction out of meeting people from different cultures, seeing them progress quickly and feeling as if they have got more power over their lives. (Language Support Worker)

When they come to us they can actually see the glimmer of light at the end of the tunnel.... Well, I think that if you can say that over the last two years that 85% of the people who have done this course are in fulltime employment, I think that that is very rewarding. You see people coming back to you saying that you changed my life - not me in particular but the course. (Vocational Support worker)

However, these services are scarce, are available only to adults, and the lack of childcare provision precludes many women from participation. The restriction of language and vocational services to those with refugee status also precludes access to most asylum-seekers. For those who complete vocational courses, but are unlikely to find high-earning jobs, the risk of losing their rent allowance also acts as a brake on entry to the labour market.

Interpreters

Interpretation and translation services are contracted by the Department of Justice, Equality and Law Reform for asylum-seekers in application interviews, appeal hearings, and criminal court appearances, though entitlement to these services is less clear in civil law proceedings, for example in child welfare proceedings.

So any interview and appeal is in the presence of an interpreter, even though they might not be needed. Even if they (asylum-seekers) have good English, an interpreter has to be there for legal purposes as well. (Interpreter)

However interpretation is not always available in the applicant's first language or dialect:

Some of them speak a language of their own and I am not familiar with it. They do speak (my language) as well, so there was never any major problem with understanding them.. (but) I think that it may be more comfortable for them to speak in their own language. Many of them would come here with a case which would incriminate the (Home Country) authorities, yet they have to speak that language. (Interpreter)

Interpreters in formal settings operate under a strict code of conduct, which requires them to offer precise translation only, without comment or advice:

One of the conditions that the Department (Justice, Equality and Law Reform) has is that we are regularly assessed....and if you do not meet their criteria they do not call you back again. They may not call you back again because of interaction with the client, demeanour, accuracy of translation...It's very impersonal work, you cannot work on a one to one level with these people, because we are not allowed to interact with them... I deal with people from my own country and I cannot talk to them.
(Interpreter)

These professional limitations may sometimes constrain the interpreter, the applicant and the application process:

A neighbour of mine that I don't know very well arrived and applied for asylum and he rang me and asked me to help him. And because of my situation I cannot do anything to help him. .. that is not ethical or professional ... He wouldn't accept it, as he said that I was a fellow (compatriot)

I think sometimes that I could help in more directions than this. All the cases depend on background information from the country. Obviously because of the situation of the asylum-seekers, the country cannot be contacted, or any authorities back in the country they have come from - (The country) shouldn't even know that these people are here. Information then cannot be gathered from the country, but I have access to newspapers published on the Internet. I could translate some of this information....Maybe I could offer that help, but I was never asked.
(Interpreter)

Communicating with and without Interpreters

Service providers in both statutory and voluntary general services find themselves increasingly challenged by the difficulty of communicating with migrants who do not speak English. Because non-nationals typically form only a small proportion of their service users, most general services have not yet begun to recruit bilingual staff, and their access to interpreters and translators is limited both by cost and by the need to offer a service here and now. Even when interpreters are available, communicating through a third party can pose difficulties. As a result, service users and providers frequently rely on other forms of impromptu communication.

What's an interpreter! ... at times we have been sent kids in taxis from the Refugee Unit: the kid would come up here and we wouldn't have access to an interpreter. We have just been doing the basics with them, drawing pictures to elicit what country they came from, what age they are, what they need.. We make sure then they will have money and somewhere to stay. It's atrocious when you're trying to do that. (Social Worker B)

Arranging for interpreters to be present, and to be briefed on the purpose and context of a meeting, can present difficulties:

We are having huge problems organising interpreters. There are agencies

who provide the service, but there is a lot of work co-ordinating access visits or meetings with somebody from this (interpreter) agency.... If the interpreter had an understanding of the kind of issues involved, and social work within the family, they would be doing their interpreting a lot better, I imagine. (Social Worker A)

Even where the interpreter is a co-professional, third party communication may be experienced as problematic in sensitive interviews:

Having done it myself before with a social worker who was doing interpreting for me with somebody who had broken English and (whose) first language was French, I remember abandoning the social worker and dealing with the person just by broken English! The social worker had perfect French, but I found it very difficult to actually communicate via another person ... they spent more time talking to the ....other social worker who had no responsibility, who had no issues at all...it was very difficult to establish a relationship with the client talking all the time through another person. (Social Worker A)

While service providers may rely on broken English and gesture to communicate and to establish a relationship with clients, they have to be cautious about presuming mutual understanding:

No one here would have (the language), but you very quickly develop a way of getting your point across. It takes a bit more time, but the...staff here would see a refugee as a challenge. No matter how clever this kid is, no matter how street wise he is, this is a kid in a foreign country with maybe an understanding of the language that he is using. The fact that he speaks English does not mean that he understands what you are thinking. He's playing with words and he's probably translating them into.... whatever language, but it doesn't mean that he has made a jump to understanding. The big worry that I would have in working with refugees is that I'm making a jump in thinking that I understand what this kid is saying. (Care Worker)

Service users without English may have to rely on acquaintances, or on their children, to translate for them when they approach services, despite their need for confidentiality and privacy:

If the child has great English and the parents have very little English, it alters the family so much and its .... dignity as well. I know of a ... woman who always had to bring her son to the doctor and that was inappropriate. I mean he was a teenager and she wanted to talk about personal issues to the doctor... (Language Support Worker)

The challenge of achieving good communication and mutual understanding, important in all services, is heightened when working with non-English speakers, and requires resources, ingenuity and sensitivity. Sometimes, mutual second languages, such as French, can be used in place of English. Service providers and service planners need to prioritise this aspect of practice, encourage bilingualism, and view proficiency in common langauges as an asset in potential employees.

Language - Practice Points

Strategies can be developed to enhance communication with service users who do not speak fluent English :

Using Interpreters

Despite their name, the task of interpreters is not to interpret, but to translate without comment except for necessary clarification. Interpreters may work for interpretation and translation agencies and be unknown to their clients, or may be relatives or acquaintances informally recruited by service users or workers.

✧ Establish that the interpreter is acceptable to the service user, for example, is of 'appropriate' gender and does not belong to a group which is not trusted.
✧ Discuss confidentiality and ensure that sensitive and personal information can be discussed safely in the interpreter's presence.
✧ Avoid using a child as interpreter, unless there is no alternative.
✧ Tell interpreters in advance about the service, the nature of the interview and emotional issues that may arise, in order to help them to translate accurately, be sensitive to the tone of the interview, and not become upset.
✧ Maintain eye contact with the service-user, rather than with the interpreter.
✧ Use simple language and allow enough time for translation.
✧ Plan follow-up contact with language in mind: get letters translated and make phonecalls when an appropriate interpreter is present.

Working without Interpreters

Do not presume automatic mutual understanding when talking with service-users who use English as a second language:

✧ Speak clearly and clarify often; if appropriate, supplement with writing, drawing and gesture.
✧ Have dictionaries, atlas and local maps available.
✧ Ask service users to write down their name or other relevant information – this promotes accuracy and can act as an ice-breaker.
✧ Give service users a card with your name and contact information, appointment dates, and details of others services to be contacted.

Team Strategies

Language issues also require collective, agency strategies :

✧ Monitor the main languages used by immigrant service-users.
✧ Develop leaflets about the service in those languages, each with English translation.
✧ Develop a short video in these languages for those who cannot read.
✧ Compile a list of official and volunteer interpreters and translators.
✧ Identify colleagues who may be able to act as occasional interpreters.
✧ Prepare cards with agency and worker names and contact information.
✧ Stock leaflets produced by N.G.O.s for refugees and asylum-seekers.
✧ Compile lists of support groups, schools, churches, health centres and other local organisations relevant to people of different origins and affiliations.

Cultural Diversity and Cultural Competence

We have a choice, and we can decide to make a society in which diversity is accepted, encouraged and made central to human practice. (Essed, 1996: viii).

As Ireland becomes a multi-ethnic and multi-faith society, a major challenge for service providers is to respond appropriately and sensitively to people with different values, expectations and customs - in other words to embrace diversity and to become culturally competent. This requires an investment in staff training and support, in developing policy, resources and co-ordination.

Policy

Statutory organisations have begun to develop policies to promote equality and cultural sensitivity. For example, in 1999, as part of the Lord Mayor of Dublin's Initiative, Dublin Corporation in partnership with the Eastern Health Board produced an information booklet on housing and welfare entitlements for refugees and asylum-seekers, in nine languages. Both organisations committed themselves to a programme of staff training on equality, anti-racism and multi-culturalism. In April 2000, The Department of Justice, Equality and Law Reform hosted a major conference on policing in a multi-cultural society. In 2001, the government is funding and coordinating a national anti-racism public awareness programme. Policy initiatives are needed at all levels within statutory and voluntary services, in order to equip workers to work effectively and inclusively with refugees and asylum-seekers and other minorities.

Training

Some N.G.O.s have responded to the growing number of non-nationals and asylum-seekers amongst their clientele by recruiting staff with foreign language skills, and by developing training and protocols for staff to help them anticipate and deal with misunderstandings that may arise from cultural differences:

We've had to give our staff some intensive language training; now we only really recruit staff that have a second language…..language training and cultural awareness and anti-racism training and things like that...

The biggest (cultural challenge) is from men from Mediterranean countries and some ... African countries (who) are not used to a tradition of having women in authority. It drives the female staff here mad. They would ask some of the men to do something and they won't do it. But then I come down and say something to them and they will do it immediately, because they don't respond to women. They also sometimes get confused…..they would be sitting down with a woman (staff member) and they are getting good attention and sometimes they would get the signals crossed and they would ask the woman out for dates and things like that, which we don't do. It's not even a sexual thing. Some of the women .. who come from...countries where there is no tradition of professional social services....tend to come in and give us gifts and ask us to their home for dinner and things like that, which we obviously don't do. And sometimes people don't understand that. So we have to be very good on our boundaries and explain. (NGO Project Leader)

Workers in statutory agencies, with only intermittent experience of working with people from different cultural groups, have traditionally had less training and support to deal with cultural differences than workers in voluntary agencies. The increasing number of workers from other countries, who have come to work in Irish statutory settings in recent years, has begun to act as a catalyst and a resource for change, and indigenous workers are also identifying their need for more training in this area.

We have no training about different people's cultures (Social Worker A)

I think (training) needs to come from within the communities, from within the culture because...only people within the culture know exactly what the culture is like.....If you have a mixed sort of organisation, we can learn from each other, and I think that is something the health board will have to look at... Other nationalities will enter the team.. and I think that would be helpful. (Social Worker C)

The employment and positioning of workers from minority cultural groups within statutory and voluntary health and welfare services needs careful thought with respect to role expectations. It should be clarified whether they are employed primarily as specialist workers and 'cultural consultants', or whether they are employed in a more generic capacity and therefore expected and entitled to carry a diverse and non-specialist workload.

Ethical Dilemmas

Lack of cultural awareness training, coupled with a statutory brief which frequently entails working with involuntary clients, can leave health board social workers uneasy or uncertain how to proceed with refugees and asylum-seekers in situations where they must investigate alleged child abuse or neglect, domestic violence or other family conflicts:

The (mother) was very open and very honest, ...she felt she's managing well and there was no need for a social worker. In relation to the physical abuse (of the children), she did not see that as a difficulty, that's her culture....Should we respond to a (refugee) family in a different way than an Irish family? I don't know whether we can or whether that is fair. But legally we have to follow through.

(In another family) There is domestic violence going on there. I spoke to the wife, but she didn't turn up. I have to go on a home visit and follow it up, because the child apparently is being hit as well. It's very difficult, because if the husband doesn't know I am coming, if he doesn't agree with me coming - I don't know about the .. culture, I think it's very much male dominant - am I putting the wife in a worse position? They are the questions you have to ask yourself all the time, yet I have to follow it up. (Social Worker C)

Faced with such uncertainties and without developed guidelines, workers

can struggle with their role, for example questioning whether they should expect non-nationals to assimilate into Irish society or whether they should adapt their own norms and practices to the circumstances of non-nationals:

Because it is different, they have come from a different culture...They have gone through a lot of turmoil... so you have to give them some leeway...some space and understanding... it is very important that they can hold on to ...their own culture...they could enrich the Irish culture. But I think it is very important for the refugees as well to be very open to the laws .. in Irish society....
Something needs to be done, work needs to be done ....maybe with all refugee families...Are the families really aware what Irish society is about... I don't know. (Social Worker C)

It may be easier for workers who work alongside asylum-seekers and other minorities on a regular basis to identify the levels of discrimination and racism that they face, and perhaps easier to develop culturally sensitive practices:

They are coming into a strange country, they have their own self-respect, their own identity, but it gets chiselled away very fast by (people) on the street that spit in their faces, shopkeepers that won't serve them, guards that keep telling them to move on... Refugees and Travellers in particular get an awful time.
.... even the people who are trying to help them are, I believe, in a lot of cases, ...patronising and discriminating against them as well... Their expectations of what these kids can achieve are very limited. The kids are being seen as spongers and in competition with Irish kids for resources .... We have a way of working here with Travellers, and it just became a natural extension that it would fit with refugees as well. The refugees always had a good relationship with the (other) kids, and that had a knock on effect with the adults as well, in not having to work on trying to get this kid to fit in. There is almost a common bond of suffering, of alienation, that makes it easier for them to mix.(Care Worker)

As this worker implies, cultural sensitivity should not be equated with 'cultural relativism': that is to say, recognition of cultural differences and different practices should not be used to justify lower standards of care and inaction by professional services.

Service providers who feel they have something to offer refugees and asylum-seekers and who have a framework for understanding their needs, even when non-nationals constitute only a minority of their clients, appear to derive considerable satisfaction from their work.

I just love dealing with people, especially people of different nationalities. They are really nice people and their resilience just amazes me. You couldn't go more down than these people are, but yet they still have this 'get up and go' that would put you to shame. (NGO Housing Support Worker)

Equity, Resources and Co-ordination

In a period of rapid social change and population growth, the need for resources is a constant preoccupation for both general and specific services. Staff shortages, work overload, and inadequate back-up services for service-users generally, can affect workers' perception of their role with refugees and asylum-seekers and raise questions of equity for other service users:

I don't advocate setting up separate services for refugees either, because then we would have a ghetto situation. The point is that the services that are already available for the Irish nationals are woefully inadequate...
(Social Worker B)

I would argue that if the system was improved for refugees, all the rest of the Irish kids would benefit from it as well. (Care Worker)

For workers in statutory agencies with a brief to protect children and who are unable to provide an adequate service for refugee minors, the problem of resources can be a source of dissatisfaction and demoralisation.

With the refugee minors, the immediate thing is accommodation and money to buy food. If it was an Irish child who was under 18, very rarely would we place them in unsupervised accommodation. ....Refugee minors are being accommodated as adults and being paid as adults. ..... they are entitled to a service from us, but we simply can't involve ourselves to the level that they need. (Social Worker D)

I mean the services that we provide already are circumscribed and limited and this has just added another layer...that is why I don't see any satisfaction in it personally. (Social Worker C)

Frustration with lack of resources leads some workers to suggest that refugees and asylum-seekers should have separate services or specialist workers:

I think some kind of ring-fenced service would be more beneficial for them for a whole variety of reasons. You might get more resources put into it and you might have people more tuned in....Having somebody (with) a background....of working with people from other cultures, or some training....and some experience of working within community care, so knowing what the issues are. I'd imagine that that would be beneficial, at least in the short term...A kind of holistic approach. (Social Worker A)

Poor co-ordination of resources and services is also a problem experienced by some service providers:

The major gap in the service is that there is meant to be co-ordination between the government departments and there clearly isn't. That would be the greatest thing.... (Care Worker)

Coordinated provision for refugees and asylum-seekers requires :
◆ Training for all service providers on multi-cultural needs and interventions
◆ Monitoring of local needs and resources among recently-arrived groups
◆ Designated specialist posts within generic services
◆ Specialist services for specific needs

Developing culturally sensitive practice in both general and specific services therefore requires investment on a number of fronts: policy, guidelines, training, support, resources and co-ordination. Individual workers cannot change services by themselves, but developing their own inter-cultural competence, challenging racist and exclusionary practices and policies, and stimulating debate within their teams are important elements in this process.

Cultural Competence : Practice Points

Cultural Competence has been defined as comprising four elements or stages: cultural awareness, cultural skill, cultural encounter and advocacy. (Northern Ireland Women's Aid Federation, 1998)[3]. Some pointers to develop cultural competence are suggested under these headings:

Cultural Awareness
✧ Become aware of your assumptions and prejudices about your own and other cultures.
✧ Gather knowledge and understanding of other cultures to help you to interact sensitively with people with different values, beliefs and practices.

Cultural Skill
✧ Approach each person with respectful curiosity.
✧ Adopt a stance of 'not knowing' – treat individuals as experts on themselves.
✧ Learn to assess the individual's cultural values, beliefs, practices, and perception of his or her situation, without relying on stereotypes.

Cultural Encounter
✧ Make opportunities to meet people from diverse backgrounds.
✧ Recognise differences between people from the same ethnic group.
✧ Look for 'cultural consultants' to help you understand minority needs.

Advocacy
✧ Make a commitment to work against the oppression of members of minorities.
✧ Identify strengths and resources that are or can be used to overcome effects of racism and discrimination. Tap into and discuss these with service users.
✧ Challenge racist attitudes and practices.
✧ Work to ensure that anti-racist policies and practices are in place.
✧ Actively seek input by minority ethnic community members in this process.

---

[3] The training pack is concerned with cultural competence in the context of domestic violence experienced by minority ethnic women and children resident in Northern Ireland, but the elements of cultural competence outlined are pertinent to work both with migrants and with those experiencing problems other than domestic violence.

An approach such as this requires openness and new thinking on the part of workers, an empowerment-based approach towards service-users, and recognition that expertise needs to be sought from the communities from which service users come. The development of cultural competence for work with minorities generally, and with refugees and asylum-seekers in particular, therefore requires a number of agency-based supports for workers:

✧ **Training :** to explore personal beliefs, especially those based on membership of a majority or privileged community; to reflect on how these beliefs influence practice; and to develop sensitivity to the circumstances and experiences of migrants from diverse ethnic minorities.

✧ **Information :** about specific ethnic / cultural minorities, and circumstances in their home countries which have led to oppression and flight.

✧ **Skill development :** opportunities to apply this awareness and knowledge with support, feedback and consultation.

✧ **Policy development :** clarity about ways in which normal agency practices, procedures and criteria for service provision may be modified for work with migrants, particularly in situations involving a conflict of interests.

✧ **Resources :** staff, space, and back-up services to meet new needs.

Health and Well-being

Health Needs

In addition to the general health needs of any diverse adult and child population, some refugees and asylum-seekers have specific health needs arising from conflict and displacement in their country of origin and from their circumstances during flight. These needs may include untreated illness or injuries, malnutrition, infectious diseases, incomplete immunisation, and require access to a range of general and specialist health services. In some cases, an urgent need for health care may be one of the push factors which prompted flight, or the basis on which humanitarian leave to remain in the host country is sought. British research has found that one in six refugees in the U.K. has a significant physical health problem (Burnett and Peel, 2001)

O'Regan (2000) suggests that one of the benefits of reception centres for Programme Refugees is the on-site availability of initial health care assessment and treatment shortly after arrival. But, for most asylum-seekers, access to health care for themselves and for their dependants is largely through mainstream health services, and access can be complicated by language barriers, referral procedures and unfamiliarity with

the structure of Irish health services. For some asylum-seekers, such as Roma 'Gypsies', a long history of institutional discrimination and oppressive practices by state services in the countries from which they have come may make them suspicious of and hesitant to use health services (Smith, 1997).

When migrants' health care needs fall into a widely stigmatised category, such as sexually transmitted diseases or addiction problems, this can cause difficulties both for those needing help and for those providing services. Asylum-seekers may fear that disclosing their health status will affect their application for refugee status or invite discrimination. Service providers may be reluctant to highlight the prevalence of such problems and the related need for resources, for fear of stigmatising asylum-seekers as a group and of fuelling negative public concerns.

Some asylum-seekers may find that the Irish climate and their living conditions produce unexpected health and dietary problems.

> *In the winter months especially….(African people) find that they get a lot of colds and chest infections; the mothers are worried about them, because they would never have had that before, and they are in hostel accommodation with a few families in one room, and it is spreading amongst them…..*
> *They are staying longer and longer in hostel accommodation; that's more frustrating … than anything else, because all they want to do… is to feed their kids their own way, to have somewhere to cook their own food. …In some B & Bs…they may be able to stay for some of the day and there may be some cooking facilities….Then again they may have to be out all day….. How can you get a proper meal for a child when you don't have cooking facilities?* (NGO Housing Support Worker)

Factors such as low income, overcrowded accommodation, lack of cooking and laundry facilities, inadequate heating and clothing, diminish the quality of life of migrants and have an adverse impact on their health. In turn, poor health, coupled with loss of extended family support, makes it more difficult to cope with family responsibilities and the uncertainties of a new life.

Mental Health

When refugees and asylum-seekers reach Ireland, many have experienced multiple losses of home, family, community, livelihood and prospects. They are also likely to have experienced trauma, such as exposure to physical and psychological threat, assault, separation, disappearance or death of loved ones. Grief, anxiety, depression, difficulty in sleeping, and post-traumatic stress are therefore widespread problems.

For some, these difficulties are incapacitating and a minority may require specialist psychiatric help. But for most, the realities of arrival in a new society, uncertain status, and the need for hard-won survival strategies to continue, mean that psychological needs are likely to be 'put on hold' until housing, income and other priorities are in place. Maslow's model of a hierarchy of human needs and the sequence of their fulfilment, from basic survival through to self-actualisation, is relevant to the situation of asylum-seekers (Maslow, 1970).

Because the asylum-seeking process is itself a stressful experience, involving uncertainty, loss, insecurity and social isolation, symptoms of psychological distress are common, but do not necessarily signify mental illness. Positive events such as confirmation of refugee status, 'leave to remain', family reunification, improvement in living conditions or increased social involvement, can do much to restore equilibrium and may transform a person's psychological and health profile. (Burnett and Peel, 2001).

Service providers therefore need to be alert to signs of distress, but also sensitive to circumstances and to the timing and acceptability of offers of counselling.

If I was to have all the resources in the world thrown at me here, I would be talking about going back and dealing with post-traumatic stress with most of them.... (We need more) psychological services.
They have to (block out their past experiences). If they are actually suffering from post-traumatic stress, it would be the most logical thing to shut it away from themselves; they probably don't want to deal with it until they are... stronger. (Care worker)

The New Day Counselling Service, set up in 1998 in conjunction with the Irish Refugee Council, provides support groups and individual counselling for refugees and asylum-seekers in Dublin. The majority of its service users have used group and individual counselling to address current concerns and difficulties, rather than traumas experienced prior to arrival. (Personal communication, 2000)

Ongoing experiences of 'acculturation stress' (Horgan, 2000), and of racism and discrimination in the host society are also strongly associated with psychological distress (Casey and O'Connell, 2000). Thus mental health problems for adults and children do not arise solely from past trauma, or from the very real difficulties of everyday living in the host society, but also from current, ongoing exposure to racist insults and attack, being snubbed or shunned, or treated in demeaning ways.

Offers of support or treatment need to be made in a culturally acceptable manner (Richman, 1998). To some refugees and asylum-seekers, whose traditional approaches to dealing with stress differ, psychological services may seem unacceptable, and stigmatising. Counselling is a westernised response to distress and may seem alien to some:

Mozambican refugees describe forgetting as their usual cultural means of coping with difficulties. Ethiopians call this 'active forgetting'.
(Summerfield, 1996, cited in Burnett and Peel, 2001)

Counselling can, however, be adapted for work with refugees, as Chris Iveson's *Postcard from Vienna,* reproduced overleaf, suggests.

Church groups, spiritual leaders or community elders may be preferred sources of support and guidance in some cultures, and it may be particularly helpful if key members of refugee communities develop

counselling skills, which they can adapt for use in supporting their members.

It is likely that, over time, more refugees and asylum-seekers will turn to Counselling, Rape Crisis and Psychiatric Services for help with past difficulties. Although these services are accustomed to responding to traumatic experiences, it is a relatively new challenge to Irish services to provide cross-cultural therapy (Krause, 1998), and to work with those who have experienced or witnessed torture, rape and injury in the course of national or internal conflicts (Levy, 1999; Sansani, 2001).

Postcard from Vienna

An application of solution-focused counselling to work with refugees.

To be Viennese and live in self-imposed exile from that beautiful European city is a high price to pay for self possession. Mrs. Bloom had vowed never to return. She was a refugee from the Nazis - except that she and thousands like her were never given the meagre welcome of refugee status. Over 50 years later her treatment as an alien still hurt. She was the only member of her family to survive the Holocaust. Ironically enough, this was probably due to the cruelty she suffered as a child. By the time the Nazis marched down her street, she was already an accomplished "survivor". She had married, had a daughter and divorced acrimoniously.

She came to see me ten years after her daughter severed contact. Mrs. Bloom was 81 and desperate to see her daughter once more before she died. Her daughter had married an Austrian and moved to Vienna. Mrs. Bloom was distraught, eaten by guilt, furiously angry, and unclear why she had come to see me.

Solution Focused Therapy

The foundation for solution-focussed therapy, which had been developed by my colleagues at the Marlborough Family Service, London and the Brief Therapy Practice, was laid by Steve deShazer and his colleagues in Milwaukee, USA, in the mid-1980s. It has two principal elements: firstly, finding out the client's goals; and secondly, finding out what he or she is doing to achieve them.

That is all, yet research in both Britain and America shows 80% of clients report significant improvement maintained over months and years. The average number of counselling sessions, irrespective of the duration or seriousness of the problem, is five.

There are many ways that clients may be invited to think creatively about their futures. One of the most useful is the miracle question: *Imagine that while you are asleep tonight there is a miracle and this problem disappears. But because you are asleep, you don't know. What will you find yourself doing tomorrow which will tell you that the problem has gone?*

This is the starting point for a detailed description of the client's wished for life and it thus becomes the goal of therapy. Interestingly enough, clients rarely come up with impossible miracles; more often than not they are entirely concrete and achievable and sometimes this description is all that is needed for the client to begin to put it into practice. Embedded in this basic principle of solution-focused work is the assumption that the client knows best and legitimate goals can only be goals which the client has defined. The assumption of the client's knowledge goes even further.

Not only is it assumed that clients know what they want. It is also assumed that they know how to achieve it. The counsellor's job is simply to help the client discover this knowledge. This discovery is made by a straightforward search for what deShazer calls exceptions. Exceptions refer to those times the problem does not appear, does not happen, or has less than an expected impact. This might be when the client gets up despite feeling depressed or when the hitherto hostile shopkeeper smiles or when the expected argument doesn't flare up. Such exceptions are usually viewed as irrelevant, merely flukes which prove rather than disprove the rule. Yet close examination of them will often reveal differences in behaviour on which future solutions can be based. Helping the client realise the significance of exceptions is one of the most important steps in solution-focused counselling. A third element and one of particular value in work with refugees and other similarly oppressed clients, is drawn from the work of Michael White and David Epston (1991).

Goals are where the client wants to get to and exceptions are what the client is already doing to get there. What is needed are the historical antecedents to the hoped for future. The life history that clients bring us is often an account of persecution, failure, despair and pain. Such a history presages a similar future and it is the horror of this future which brings the client into counselling. However, these histories are only one version of each client's life; a selection of events which put together form pattern which makes sense. If life stories are sufficiently analysed, then it is not difficult to draw out different threads and different patterns. Most refugees have submerged stories of perseverance, determination, survival, hope and even humour. When such stories are brought into the light, what appeared as random exceptions are quickly recognised as alternative ways of living and what seemed distant dreams are no more than the logical development of a worthwhile life.

An Eritrean Story

Amarat and Abram were from Eritrea and spoke no English. Amarat had tried to strangle her 9-year old son and been compulsorily admitted to a psychiatric hospital. Abram was taken into care. I first saw them a few days after Amarat's discharge from hospital. Both sat with their heads bowed and while Amarat would at least attempt to answer my questions, Abram steadfastly refused. Even with an excellent interpreter (who said solution-focused therapy fitted very well with Eritrean ideas of life and problem-solving) it was being clearly demonstrated that no matter how good the questions, they were meaningless outside the context of a trusting relationship. These, however, are not necessarily ones built up over a long period of time. When clients know they are being listened to and treated

with respect, they will listen to and answer questions. If the questions help them discover new things about themselves, then the counselling will start being effective.

This process need only take minutes. With Amarat, I adapted an idea of de Shazer's which is to use scales to help clients measure change. On a blackboard I drew a hillside and asked if there were were hills in Amarat's part of Eritrea. For the first time she smiled and said there were. She said her only aim at present was to return to good health and I asked her to write "good health" in Tigrinia (her first language) at the top of the hill and "hospital" at the bottom. I then asked her to place herself on the hill. She put herself one third of the way up. This already showed that she saw herself improving and I might have spent time asking about these "exceptions". Instead, I asked her to show where she would be tomorrow. She moved another third of the way up the hill. Just as the third she had already moved represented these things she was already doing to reach her goal, the third she would move "by tomorrow" represented the next stage of her journey towards her goal. Eliciting a description of the behaviour that would make the difference would be the same as describing the next stage of the solution —and it would all have come from Amarat.

I asked her
"What will need to happen for you to move from here on the mountain to here where you will be tomorrow?"
She gave her first extended response: *"I will put behind me these memories and frustrations which fill my mind and when they come, I will leave my room and walk. I will do other things to make drive the thoughts away. I like cooking and shopping. This is what I am already doing and it is helping me to become well. I will just do more of it".*

In the second session with Amarat and Abram, we used the mountain to trace the course of mother and son's hoped for rehabilitation. In the third, we traced their family history, learned of life in their village and something of the extraordinary story of their escape and survival. As they spoke, they grew. They actually filled more of the space around them as they replaced a story of fear, weakness, running away and desertion with one of courage, protection, friendship, determination, and survival. This is not to say that the first story was abandoned altogether, nor that both stories were not primarily stories of loss and pain. It is just that in a foreign and largely hostile country, they had been vulnerable in believing only the negative accounts of their lives and by forgetting the story of their strength and achievement, they were forgetting what they knew about surviving hard times and resolving difficult problems.

The fourth and last session simply reviewed the many changes made in the three months we had been meeting and the plans were laid for Abram's return home. A year later, Amarat and Abram both speak English, Abram is doing well in school and Amarat has found work as a cleaner. Their lives are far from easy but they are living them with increased confidence.

As for Mrs. Bloom, I met her three times before she wrote cancelling our appointment. With Mrs. Bloom, I had been unable to establish a picture of her life when the goal of seeing her daughter was reached. Each time we moved towards a description she would be reminded of all the injustices done to her by her husband and daughter and this would remind her of the injustices she had done to them. She would then castigate herself and the whole account would be linked to the loss of her family in the Holocaust and another cycle of horror, injustice, and anger would unfold. As I listened to these accounts, I looked for opportunities to hint at counter-stories; the evidence of love, commitment, decisiveness, determination, achievement, survival and so on. She ended her meetings with me because I had become too wedded to the "alternative story" and so failed to take account of her pain and guilt. I felt terrible and wrote her a short note apologising for not listening well enough. And I added a PS - "If you ever get to Vienna, send me a postcard".

Six weeks later I received a postcard from Vienna saying only *"All is well"*.

Included here by kind permission of the author, **Chris Iveson.**

Previously published in *The Irish Social Worker* 16.3. Summer 1998, pp. 21-22.

Gender, Age and Health

The experience of those working in refugee camps with women refugees, who have experienced gender-based violence - rape, domestic violence or female genital mutilation - prior to or in the camps, suggests not only that support should be provided by female workers, but also that refugee women should be recruited and trained as health workers, and that women should be consulted about the form that services for them will take. (U.N.H.C.R., 1991)

Women asylum-seekers who access mainstream health services in the host country can also face particular barriers, including:
◆ inappropriate interpreters for discussion of sensitive health problems
◆ difficulty with being examined or treated by male health professionals
◆ insensitivity to the specific cultural implications of their health problems
◆ lack of child care support to facilitate attending health professionals
◆ lack of a female support network with whom to discuss health decisions
◆ differences in gynaecological or obstetric practices
◆ fear that disclosing domestic violence or other family problems will affect their own or partner's asylum application, or exacerbate tension in the home.

Whilst the majority of refugees and asylum-seekers are relatively young and healthy, a minority are older and may have particular health concerns, such as:
◆ language barriers and prolonged reliance on others to communicate and discuss their health problems
◆ disrupted treatment of existing health problems
◆ unfamiliar or unwelcome medical treatment
◆ periods in hospital without familiar people who speak their language
◆ anxiety about growing old, dying and being buried in a foreign country.

Over time, as the number of older refugees settling in Ireland increases, such problems and concerns are likely to become more widespread. Knowledge that some elderly Holocaust survivors have experienced a resurgence of anxiety and depression related to war-time trauma also suggests that the mental health needs of older migrants will become more visible and pressing.

Thus gender, age and family status need to be recognised as significant factors in health risk and in ease of access to appropriate services.

Health – Practice Points

✧ Asylum-seekers are disempowered by the events preceding, during and following their flight. Adopt an empowering approach.
✧ Work to reduce language barriers and seek acceptable interpreters.
✧ Be sensitive to gender, age and cultural issues in assessment and treatment.
✧ Be sensitive about the timing and acceptability of treatment and counselling.
✧ Prioritise material and living conditions which contribute to poor health.
✧ Ensure that health care is accompanied by information, in relevant languages, about rights and resources.
✧ Consult with members of the refugee community on ways to improve the targeting and delivery of health services.

Children and Families

Sources of stress

Asylum-seekers may arrive alone or accompanied. Those who are alone face particular isolation and loneliness; those with family members, whilst buffered against isolation, may be acutely anxious for their dependants and coping with changing family roles. Whether alone or accompanied, asylum-seekers begin life in Ireland anxious about those left behind and about the future.

Richman (1998) describes the experience of child refugees and asylum-seekers as like being in the 'midst of a whirlwind' : swept from the familiar to the unfamilar, in a bewildering and stressful sequence of events. A key factor in maintaining the well-being of migrant children in the face of this disruption is continuity of care by their parents or by guardians to whom they are attached. Some children, however, have lost family members, have become separated, or have been sent ahead for safety, and may arrive in the care of a relative or unfamiliar person or unaccompanied: for these children, the disruption and stress associated with flight and arrival are greater.

Identity

For all migrants, arrival in a new country brings questions of identity to the fore. Taken for granted assumptions about self and others are challenged and the experience of becoming an 'Other', even temporarily, is foregrounded. For those whose migration was prompted by persecution and conflict, and who cannot predict if, or when, they will return to their own country, identity issues can be particularly problematic or ambivalent.

Becoming a refugee presents both adults and children with questions about who they are and where they belong, because they have lost the surety of their place in the world. (Richman, 1998: 31)

Insecurity about the future can make children cling to the first place they reach and each subsequent move of accommodation or school may be disturbing. Adult migrants too may look for emotional anchors: they may choose to emphasise their religious or cultural practices or political beliefs more strongly than before, in order to maintain their sense of identity and kinship with others. However, this can sometimes prove problematic for their children, who may be attempting to reconcile two cultures, at home and in school.

Over time, if they remain in their new country, most adults and children will move gradually towards a 'bi-cultural identity'. Children typically make this move more quickly than adults, as they learn English and integrate into school and local networks. However, for children to develop a bi-cultural identity which values both cultures, they need some continuity with their own language and culture and to learn about their family history, country of origin and the events which led to their migration.

Parents, older siblings and relatives are children's primary resource in this process, as 'culture-keepers' and family historians, and while they may understandably wish to protect children from the most distressing aspects of their past, can be encouraged to share other information, memories and stories.

For children with no photos or mementoes of their former life, it can be helpful to draw pictures, make a memory book about their life before they migrated, or to write letters to loved ones who have died or from whom they are separated.

Schools also have an important role to play in supporting children's engagement with their own language and culture and in promoting an ethos of pluralism and multi-culturalism in the classroom (Richman, 1998)[4].

Class-mates and teachers may also support asylum-seeking children through difficult experiences, such as refusal of asylum applications, and raise consciousness in the school about immigration and its implications. (Ward, 2000)

Current and past problems

Whilst past traumas and the disruption of flight clearly impact on children's development, what happens to them subsequently in the host country is

---

[4]
Richman explores in some detail ways in which schools can help refugee children. See especially chapters 10 and 11.

equally important. Negative experiences, such as parental distress, family conflict, disruptive moves of accommodation, difficulty in school, rejection by other children, or racist behaviour by strangers, compound earlier adversity. Positive experiences, such as family support, relationships with other caring adults and achievement in school do much to mitigate its effects. Workers engaged in assessment with refugee or asylum-seeking children should take account of both past and present circumstances, in order to understand the child's needs and difficulties. This dual-focused approach to assessment applies also in work with parents and families.

Child Protection

The difficulties of identifying children at risk and protecting them from abuse or neglect can be compounded in the case of migrant children by language barriers, difficulty in gathering accurate information, and uncertainty about the weight to be given to cultural differences in child-rearing practices.

Examples of situations where dilemmas may arise include the following:
- ◆ Children left unattended by adults for lengthy periods, where this seems to have been accepted in their country of origin.
- ◆ Children accompanying adults who are begging or selling in school hours or in dangerous places.
- ◆ The use of severe discipline by otherwise caring and capable parents, who regard such disciplinary measures as normal, acceptable and necessary.
- ◆ Generational conflicts, where parents disapprove of their children's desires to behave like their peers, and which lead to punishment, curfews, or children running away. Girls are more likely to experience these conflicts.
- ◆ Disagreements between parents and health professionals about appropriate treatment for a sick or disturbed child.

The challenge in such situations is to combine a central focus on the child's needs with respect for the parents' culture and circumstances.

The material and environmental pressures to which families are subjected, such as inadequate finances, overcrowded or dangerous accommodation, and lack of cooking or washing facilities, should also be clearly represented in any child protection assessment. Workers may need to adopt advocacy measures.

Child Protection Practice Points:

✧ Aim for the best assessment of child and family in the circumstances and acknowledge gaps in information.
✧ Minimise language and communication barriers.
✧ Be sensitive to children's difficulties in talking about conflict or abuse: eg: loyalty to family members and the impact of past experiences[5].

---

[5] One of the professionals interviewed for this training pack mentioned a case where a teenage girl disclosed sexual abuse, but reacted badly to the suggestion that the Gardaí be informed - it transpired that she had previously been sexually assaulted by police in her home country.

- ◇ Clarify agency role and brief, and its distinction from asylum procedures.
- ◇ Be honest with parents about the basis of concerns for the child.
- ◇ Explore parents' views of these concerns and their solutions.
- ◇ Take account of past and current stressors which affect parenting and family stability; acknowledge their resilience in coping with traumatic events and attempting to keep their children safe.
- ◇ Show respect for parents –not discussing parenting difficulties in front of the child, or interviewing the child without their knowledge, unless essential.
- ◇ Seek culturally appropriate support and preventive measures which may reduce current and future risk.

Children in Care

Migrant children may need alternative care in a number of circumstances:
- ◆ Separated or unaccompanied children
- ◆ Breakdown in family or care arrangements
- ◆ Parental death or illness
- ◆ Child protection concerns
- ◆ Children who leave home

In such situations, placement in care is likely to occur on an emergency basis. The sense of dislocation experienced by most children who come into care is compounded for refugee and asylum-seeking children by being cut off from their already disrupted culture, roots and community. They are unlikely to be placed with foster parents who share their ethnic background, language or religion, and in residential units may feel inhibited about displaying differences.

Their cultural identity is a major problem. There is so much pressure on them to blend in, that they cannot practice their own cultural stuff here. no-one is preventing them from practising their culture or religion, but there is so much pressure that they daren't do it. (Care Worker)

Basic information about their age, origins and family members may be missing. Unaccompanied children in particular often fear that disclosing personal information in order to trace family members at home will endanger them.

If a kid has parents imprisoned in certain countries... once a social worker here begins to try to source family information about the kid, we hear of retaliations against the parents in prison...It's almost as if the parents are hostages. (Care Worker)

Care Placements - Practice Points

- ◇ Assessment may need to begin with the child's state and circumstances at the point of placement, rather than with a family history. Over time, the child may feel able to disclose more details safely.
- ◇ The aim of reuniting the child with his or her family is central, but care planning may have to proceed in the absence of contact or family work.
- ◇ White foster parents and care workers need training and support to help

Integrating: Saint Mary's Boys National School, Dublin. March 2001
Photographer: Derek Speirs / Report.

their children to deal with racism and to develop a positive self image[6].

✧ The child's need for psychological support is likely to be considerable, in view of past experiences and current dislocation.
✧ Integration into a sympathetic school as rapidly as possible provides structure and routine and opportunities for achievement and social contact.
✧ Involvement in youth clubs and refugee groups from the same country help to overcome isolation and to support cultural identity.
✧ Attention should be paid to the religious or spiritual needs of children and young people from diverse cultures.
✧ Many asylum-seeking young people have spent time living independently or homeless and behave, or are treated, as if they were much older. This premature maturity should not detract from recognising their need for support and protection.

Separated and Unaccompanied Children

The Separated Children in Europe Programme (1999) defines 'separated children' as:

...children under 18 years of age who are outside their country of origin and separated from both parents, or their legal / customary primary caregiver. Some.. are totally alone while others... may be living with extended family members. All such children are separated children and entitled to international protection under a broad range of international and regional instruments. Separated children may be seeking asylum because of fear of persecution or due to armed conflict or disturbances in their own country, or they may be the victims of trafficking for sexual or other exploitation, or they may have travelled to Europe to escape conditions of serious deprivation. (Section 2.1.)

The Separated Children in Europe Programme uses the word 'separated' rather than 'unaccompanied' because it better defines the essential problem that such children face...that they are without the care and protection of their parents or legal guardians and as a consequence suffer socially and psychologically from this separation. While some separated children appear to be 'accompanied' when they arrive in Europe, the accompanying adults are not necessarily able or suitable to assume responsibility for their care. (Section 2.3.)

Children and young people who arrive alone, or accompanied by people other than their usual carers, are therefore particularly vulnerable. Separation from family members, bereavement, loneliness, anxiety for themselves and fear for loved ones, involve acute emotional distress.

---

[6] Issues arising for white carers of black or mixed-race children are addressed in a number of recent British studies. See for example: The Scottish Office (1998), *Valuing Diversity.*

> **"Go and Ask for Justice"**
>
> *When 17-year old Olu arrived into...Dublin airport last December, she had no idea where she was. She'd flown through the night from Nigeria.... with a man she knew only as Patrick. At Arrivals, he turned to her" "Go and ask for Justice" he said. Then he disappeared into the crowd ... 'They killed my mother and my baby sister. My father brought me and my four brothers to our village to hide...Then my father came and told me to follow Patrick. He didn't say where I was going. He said not to talk to anyone on the way'....... What Olu wants is to be reunited with her father and brothers in Nigeria. But she doesn't know where they are, or if they are okay.....'If I'd known it was just going to be me here, I'd never have come'.*
> (McKay, 2000) [7]

Following arrival, many separated young people find themselves thrust into prematurely adult roles. They may be placed in B & B or hostel accommodation, organise their own food and finances, find a school which will accept them, cope with homework and language difficulties, and their asylum application - without the support of a guardian.

In 2000 alone, over 500 unaccompanied young people sought asylum in Ireland, and a social work team to support and guide them through the legal process was recruited by the East Coast Area Health Board. The Vincentian Refugee Centre in Phibsboro, Dublin, also provides practical and emotional support to a small number of separated young people. However, many cope without professional support, legal advice or 'go missing'. (Haughey, 2001)

As the quotations from professionals earlier in this chapter show, recognition of the gaps in services for these vulnerable young people is particularly frustrating for workers in child care services, and raises questions of equity in treatment of children from indigenous and non-indigenous backgrounds.

Separated Children – Practice Points

The Separated Children in Europe Programme (1999) sets out a number of principles for working with separated children, which are supported by international legal conventions, and which provide a guide to good practice for all agencies. These include the following.

⬦ The 'best interests of the child' precede all other considerations, including immigration status, and they should never be detained for reasons related to their immigration status.
⬦ Separated children are entitled to the same rights and treatment (accommodation, education, training, health care, language support etc) as national children, and should be treated first and foremost as children.
⬦ Their views and wishes must be taken into account in decisions about them.

---

[7] Susan McKay provides extended profiles of two young people arriving unaccompanied in Dublin. Brief extracts from one of these profiles are condensed here.

- Decisions should be timely and take account of their long-term interests and welfare.
- They must be enabled to maintain their mother tongue and links with their culture and religion.
- They must be provided with suitable interpreters who speak their preferred language when they are interviewed or need access to services, and interviews should be conducted in a child-friendly manner.
- Information should not be disclosed which could endanger the child's family members in the home country. The child's consent should be sought before disclosing sensitive information to other organisations or individuals.
- A Guardian or adviser should be appointed as soon as possible after arrival to advise and protect the child, to ensure that the child has suitable legal representation, to advocate on the child's behalf and to explore the possibility of family tracing and reunification.
- Interim needs for accommodation and education should take priority and should be based on an assessment.
- Siblings should be kept together unless they wish otherwise.
- Once a separated child or young person is allowed to remain, a careful assessment is needed to plan for their care or 'after-care'.
- Government departments and services should co-operate to ensure that the welfare and rights of separated children are protected and enhanced.
- All professionals working with separated children need appropriate training.

Conclusion

Harrell-Bond (1999) reflects that one of the major sources of stress for refugees may be the experience of being helped in a markedly unequal relationship between helper and recipient. Whereas most Second World War refugees received minimal assistance and were left to establish a new life for themselves, modern refugees are managed, regulated and provided for to a far greater degree. Drawing on her own and other people's experience of refugee camps and of resettlement processes in host countries, Harrell-Bond points to the damaging effects of 'refugee' stereotypes, of reduced status, of enforced dependency, and of the requirement to be grateful for assistance.

Is the common experience of suffering loss of status or 'declassing' in relation to helpers another source of stress for refugees? Perhaps for most refugees in the world, the first time they receive rations in a camp or 'dole' money from a state institution may also be the first time in their lives they have received help from a stranger...
Rather than viewing themselves as heroes who have stood up to, and escaped from oppressive regimes, today many refugees are very reluctant to admit their status. Rather than perceiving themselves as persons who have rights under international humanitarian and human rights law, many feel they are obligated for any help they receive.
(Harrell-Bond, 1999: 143.)

If the delivery of aid and assistance to refugees and asylum-seekers carries such risks, the way in which services are delivered is of critical importance.

The challenge to service providers in both statutory and voluntary agencies is to combine the provision of needed services with:

✧ cultural sensitivity
✧ inclusiveness
✧ respect
✧ empowerment
✧ the expertise of refugee organisations
✧ development of policy and resources
✧ contribution to positive discourses about flight and migration.

Key readings

Alger, A. (ed)(1999), *Refugees: Perspectives on the Experience of Forced Migration,* London: Cassell.

MacLachlan, M. and O'Connell, M. (eds) (2000), *Cultivating Pluralism: Psychological, Social and Cultural Perspectives on a Changing Ireland.* Dublin: Oak Tree Press

Northern Ireland Women's Aid Federation (1998), *Violence on the Edge: exploring the needs of minority ethnic women at risk of domestic violence in Northern Ireland.* N. Ireland Women's Aid Federation / Training for Women Network Ltd.

Richman, N. (1998), *In the Midst of the Whirlwind: A Manual for Helping Refugee Children.* London: Trentham Books.

Separated Children In Europe Programme (1999), *Statement of Good Practice.* Geneva: U.N.H.C.R. / Save the Children Alliance.

U.N.H.C.R. (1991), *Guidelines on the Protection of Refugee Women.* Geneva.

Scenarios for discussion

Scenario 1

Refugees and asylum-seekers are often described as 'ordinary people in extraordinary circumstances'. This formulation aims to heighten awareness of our assumptions about, and our responses to, refugees and asylum-seekers.

How do 'ordinary people in extraordinary circumstances' challenge our services:

- *practice?*
- *waiting lists?*
- *procedures?*

Scenario 2

You are working in a small but well-respected non-statutory agency, which until recently has dealt only with Irish service-users. In recent times, an increasing number of people from 'new communities' has been attending the service.

What does your agency / team need to do in order to:

- *develop policy?*
- *initiate training ?*
- *monitor practice?*

Scenario 3

For the first time in your professional career you are employed in a social work agency which works with service users from diverse ethnic backgrounds.

List what, for you, will be the major challenges to your:
- *knowledge base*
- *skills*
- *practice*
- *attitudes and beliefs*

and identify what:
- *you can keep and build on*
- *you need to abandon*
- *pressing training needs you have as a result of this changing work context*

Scenario 4

How do you and your team deal with the following issues when they arise among refugee / asylum-seeker communities? :

- *Domestic violence*
- *Problematic alcohol use*
- *Drug use*
- *Homelessness*
- *Child Protection issues*

- If you have experience dealing with these issues, compare and contrast the response you and your team make when dealing with Irish national and with non-nationals?
- If you have not had such experience, brainstorm how your practice might differ?

Scenario 5

You are a medical social worker in a general hospital, where several patients have been referred to you because they are asylum-seekers. Some have special needs, but others have no obvious reason for referral other than their refugee / asylum-seeker status.

- What special needs might the first group of patients have, and how would you respond?

- How would you respond to the second group, who are referred despite coping well?

- How would you deal with the issue of inappropriate referrals?
  Liaison with other professionals?
  New criteria for referral? If so, what criteria?
  Other strategies? If so, what strategies?

Scenario 6

It is reported that many asylum-seekers have to live in substandard conditions:- Hostels and Bed and Breakfast accommodation that are sometimes very crowded, with poor facilities, inadequate hot water or heating; that require residents to leave for long periods each day, or to return early in the evening or risk losing their place. When residents complain, they may be asked "What do you expect?"

- As a social worker, how would you intervene and advocate on behalf of asylum-seekers in this situation?

Scenario 7

Adopting (a) a strengths perspective
    and   (b) community development principles,
consider how you would set about developing the following resources for
refugees and asylum-seekers in your catchment area:

◆ *A Peer-Support group?*
◆ *A Community Mothers' Scheme?*
◆ *A Family Support Service?*

What issues would you need to confront?

CHAPTER FIVE :

PRINCIPLES FOR INDIVIDUAL AND ORGANISATIONAL PRACTICE

Introduction

Chapter One reviewed a number of different theoretical perspectives and frameworks, upon which practitioners can draw in order to address the needs of minority groups, and specifically the needs of refugees and asylum-seekers. Frameworks should be chosen carefully and the implications of adopting a specific framework understood and considered, as outlined in Chapter One.

Chapters Two and Three, which review the legal and practical issues that refugees and asylum-seekers face, and Chapter Four which reviews service provision highlight the extent to which the needs of refugees and asylum-seekers are only beginning to be addressed in Ireland. Chapter Five is concerned with practice responses to those needs and the principles which underlie them.

Remaining mindful of the ethical base underlying social work, and of the dual responsibility of social workers to attend to both the environmental and personal dimensions of service users' lives, it is possible to articulate some guiding principles for good practice, both for the individual practitioner and for the agency.

Key concepts in intercultural work

Culture

Cultures may be considered as models or designs for living. We are all heavily influenced by the cultures that we are exposed to, brought up in, adopt or reject, and cultures influence us on many different levels.

Levels of cultural influence include:

◆ Self-culture - which develops and is specific to our most unique, personal experiences.
◆ A culture of family - exemplified and experienced between ourselves and those who were or are our most immediate caretakers and nurturers.
◆ A culture of sameness - experienced by those who are similar in characteristics of ethnicity, language, custom and belief.
◆ A 'mini' culture of influence - experienced by those who share a particular condition, status or interest , which may be temporary or life-long.
◆ A local or regional culture - experienced in one's community or region of residence - rural, urban or suburban. For example, the 'West', the 'North', the 'Midlands' are seen to share distinctive characteristics.
◆ A socio-political, society-wide culture, which often espouses a set of dominant, national norms of behaviour that may be overarching and have pervasive influence upon each citizen of an entire nation. These

influences are often articulated and operationalised through prevailing forms of constitutional government, social institutions and philosophies addressing societal goals. (McGrath & Axelson 1993)

Values

Interpersonal and intergroup relations are influenced by people's perceptions of others. Values, part of our internal selves, structure our perceptions, and chart out past and present course. Values help explain our nature and our behaviour. What we value can be an idea, belief, practice, or anything that is important to or desired by us. Values are also influenced by normative rules of conduct external to us, and constitute the things we hold in common as members of a group or culture. The way that certain common basic needs are satisfied and how values are defined tend to be related to our group membership.

Quantity and Quality of Multicultural Contacts

Our ability to relate effectively to any event or person we experience is influenced by the quantity and the quality of experiences we have had with similar events or persons. Based on the quality and quantity of such exposure, we develop a reservoir of information and ways of relating to such people and events.

If we have had limited opportunities to meet with, work with, and get to know certain groups, we are more reliant on the media and external sources of information. This may result in negative images or stereotypes being associated with that particular group. Similarly, if we have few contacts with members of a particular group, but these contacts are generally negative, then it is more likely that our perceptions of this group will be negative and shape behaviour which will have a negative influence on future contacts with members of that group.

The influence of Stereotypes

A stereotype is a generalised and usually simplified conceptualisation or belief about another person or people, place or thing. Stereotypes are commonly used to identify and describe others and so have major influence on our perception of others. The use of stereotypical statements to describe persons different from ourselves, particularly when not contradicted, reinforces already existing notions about the nature of other persons or groups.

Stereotypes are so commonly used, that we can easily begin to think they are true. Without sufficient experience with others of difference, it can be very difficult for us to distinguish what is useful and true about others from what is neither truthful nor useful. Stereotypes are not useful, and can be positively damaging, when they perpetuate negative images of groups which justify a discriminatory or oppressive stance.

The Individual Response

The role of the helping professional

The overall aim of helping professionals can be said to be *'to assist clients to search for and reach their desired goals'*.

A professional helping relationship is ideally a co-equal relationship, in which both client and helper co-participate, co-determine and co-authorise what will be done in an effort that validates and empowers the service user. Intercultural work requires the worker to accept the partiality of his or her knowledge and skill, and to emphasise and elicit the knowledge and skill of the service user in order to determine how best the helping process should proceed.

The cultural constructs we develop over time, shaped by family, friends, societal experiences and media images, influence the directions and goals we support service users to move toward. But what happens when service users' experiences and expectations differ from those of helpers? The challenge for the worker then is to establish a process with the service user, whereby the service user's meaning, experiences and expectations are elicited. A simple step is to start an interview by asking:

'tell me what is happening for you now and how would you like me to help you?' (adapted from Fook, 2000),

This sets the tone for active listening by the worker to the service user's experience. It can be argued that the reality of achieving service user goals is directly related to our understanding of the service user's world.

Principles for Multicultural Practice on an Individual Level

✧ Become aware of dimensions of each service user's experiences in relation to race or ethnicity; socio-economic status; religion, language, education, gender, generation, geographic region, physical condition or status, and community residence.

✧ Develop awareness of the effects of this information on yourself.

✧ Examine the differences within the difference. (All Travellers are not alike; all refugees are not alike; all black people are not alike).

✧ Adopt a stance of 'not knowing': you have expertise on particular matters and you want to be of help to this service user, but this person is expert on him or her self and you need his/her help in matching the two.

✧ Do not assume that your client will understand the nature of social work agencies and the social control functions Social Workers often hold. Explain.

✧ Approach each service user with respectful curiosity, as an individual with a unique value and cultural map.

✧ Know your own limitations: identify when it is appropriate to seek specialist help for service users, or 'cultural consultants' who can help you to be more sensitive to the needs of those who differ.

✧ Identify strengths and resources that exist both in the individual and in emerging community groups, which can be utilised to help overcome the effects of racism and discrimination. Actively tap into and discuss these with service users.

✧ Accept that racism and discrimination occur in Irish society today. Retain a role as advocate for your client and use your strength in, and familiarity with, Irish society to challenge racism and discrimination. It is valid to see yourself as champion to those who suffer oppression, provided you also recognise and draw on the strengths and resources that minority communities contain.

✧ Examine organisational and agency policies and practices which can unthinkingly have racist or discriminatory effects. Does a 'difference-blind' approach exist? Can you act as an advocate for change along with members of different minority groups, to ensure that services and policies become more responsive to differential needs? Can you form a coalition with others for change?

Service Provision and the Organisational Response – towards Equality Proofing

John Richards, a Director of Social Services in Northern Ireland, has developed a framework for analysis and change on an organisational level in relation to what is now called 'equality proofing'; that is, the extent to which the practices and policies of an organisation either comply with or run counter to principles of equality.

I believe that if service providers are going to truly meet the needs of people from different racial groups, they need to take responsibility and action in five key areas. These are:
◆ *policy and planning*
◆ *service delivery and customer care*
◆ *recruitment and selection*
◆ *staff development and training*
◆*highlighting and disseminating good practices* (Richards, 1999 : 1)

Each of these areas will be considered in turn and, drawing on Richards' original work, suggestions made as to how these areas might be addressed in the Irish context.

1.   Policy and Planning

✧ There should be in place for all service providers and service users a written policy on racial equality.
✧ For statutory authorities, this should be endorsed by senior managers and their public Boards and Government Departments.

- ✧ For non-statutory organisations, the policy should be endorsed by management committees and boards.
- ✧ The policy should be drawn up in consultation with service users from minority groups or, if minority groups are not yet specific service users, from potential service users within minority groups.
- ✧ Comprehensive minority monitoring systems should be established. Wherever possible, social care providers should extend their policy and practice requirements to those supplying services through contracting procedures. This means that voluntary groups contracted to provide services (for example, St Michael's House for learning disabilities; St. John Of God for psychiatric services) would also be required to adopt the written policy, or to devise their own version.
- ✧ A racial equality policy should acknowledge and provide for multiple oppressions, which can occur on grounds of sex, age, disability or sexual orientation.
- ✧ Racial equality objectives should be further underpinned in organisations by incorporating such objectives in job descriptions, and in staff appraisal and promotion processes.
- ✧ Organisations can learn about good practice in other organisations through networking with each other on their policy and practice in this area.

'As countries are beginning to respond more robustly to different racial groups we can benefit enormously from the good and not-so-good experiences of others' (Richards, 1999, p. 2).

A race equality statement should contain:

- ✧ A commitment by the agency to be anti-racist and non-discriminatory.
- ✧ A commitment to the recruitment of more ethnic minority staff at all levels, and details on how this will be achieved.
- ✧ The promotion of positive actions in service delivery for people from ethnic minorities in a culturally appropriate manner, and an undertaking to reward such initiatives, for example through bonus or prize systems.
- ✧ A system for developing a network of contacts with ethnic minority groups, in order to increase knowledge, awareness and understanding of different cultures, and a system for facilitating the dissemination of such knowledge through publications, joint presentations and co-working.
- ✧ Effective, continuous monitoring and evaluation of service provision to people from ethnic minorities, following consultation with members of ethnic minorities on how such monitoring should be implemented.

2. Service Delivery and Service-User Care

✧ One of the first things providers need to know is who in which minority communities are accessing services, and whether minority communities which are potential service users are not availing of the service and why. There can be a significant difference between the numbers of referrals of people from minority communities and the take-up of service, and this may suggest that service providers have failed at the first stage – the referral stage.

- ✧ It is important therefore to monitor service delivery at all stages –potential referrals, actual referrals, assessment and service delivery.
- ✧ Complaints procedures for service users need to be equally accessible to members of minority groups.
- ✧ Services should have consultation mechanisms to establish the needs and level of satisfaction of ethnic minority service users.
- ✧ Translation and interpreting services should be available to ensure that ethnic minority service users have full access to services. Information leaflets should be available in a variety of languages.
- ✧ Managers and staff responsible for service delivery must take account of culture, histories and relationships, and adapt their thinking accordingly without falling into the trap of 'cultural relativism' whereby all practices, if culturally appropriate, are seen as being of equal value.
- ✧ The differing dietary and sometimes cosmetic requirements of ethnic minority groups need to be considered in the delivery of services. Staff should be accepting of these needs and facilitate their provision.

3. Recruitment and Selection

Guidelines for non-discriminatory recruitment practices need to be drawn up by employers, understood and implemented correctly by all involved in recruitment and selection. The Equality Authority in Dublin is likely to be the key agency to offer guidance on these matters. Specific aspects highlighted by Richards (1999) include:

- ✧ The need for employers to consider how they can target publicity for vacancies and opportunities to the widest selection pool across different communities and minority groups.
- ✧ The need to take specific steps to encourage ethnic minority candidates to apply for jobs in areas where they are under-represented.
- ✧ The need for employers to collect, collate and use data on applicants by ethnic origin and ensure that they use interview questions on racial equality.
- ✧ Personnel and recruitment units could consider using race equality targets for all grades, professions and teams, perhaps with explicit timetables.
- ✧ Codes of Practice which are developed by employment equality units should be adopted and implemented.

4. Staff Development and Training

Staff development and training are now recognised as an important activity in most major social service and health care organisations. Staff induction courses serve as a particularly important point at which agency commitment to racial equality can be outlined and demonstrated.

Particular aspects of personnel policy need to be reviewed, in order to assess whether procedures are fair and effective across minority groups. Richards (1999) identifies the following as matters for review:

- ♦ grievance procedures
- ♦ disciplinary procedures
- ♦ response to racial attacks and harassment
- ♦ staff appraisals
- ♦ provision for religious and cultural needs
- ♦ health and safety policy.

Service providers could consider the following questions:

- ♦ Do existing programmes of development and training meet the needs of ethnic minority staff?
- ♦ Are additional programmes needed to enhance the skills and career development of ethnic minority staff?
- ♦ Are managers trained to implement race equality action plans and programmes?
- ♦ Are there any concerns about high levels of dismissal or resignation by particular individuals at particular levels – and if so should exit interviews be conducted with those who leave the agency?

Richards (1999) emphasises that the onus is on employers to be pro-active in developing fair employment and career progression schemes for all staff.

5. Public Promotion of Equality Practices

- ✧ Service providers should both implement equal opportunities policy in practice and represent themselves publicly as doing so.
- ✧ Agency staff need to be provided with information on equality legislation and codes of practice.
- ✧ Equality practices and policies should be highlighted both within the agency and outside, so that all staff, applicants for jobs, potential applicants, service users, community groups, and the general public are aware of the policies in place and of the ways in which the agency is implementing its race equality policies. Richards (1999) suggests that service providers should:

> *draw out the implications of racial equality in staff handbooks, recruitment literature, induction training and other publications on service delivery. They should provide their statement of commitment to racial equality in advertisements, recruitment materials and procedures...Public information materials should reflect social equality and cultural diversity in text and illustrations. (Richards 1999:5)*

- ✧ Service providers should also consider using the media to highlight good practice and to reflect the ethnic and racial diversity of service providers and service users. Those from minority groups should not remain 'hidden' staff or users of the service. Successful equality work should be promoted in the media. Ethnic minority media channels should also be identified and used.

Conclusion

Building on Resilience and Advocating for Equality and Inclusion

Resilience comprises a set of qualities that help a person to withstand many of the negative effects of adversity (Gilligan, 2001, p. 5).

Refugees and asylum-seekers face many stresses and adversities before, during and after the asylum-seeking and the longer-term resettlement process. Resilience can be promoted by provision of positive, supportive experiences alongside or following adverse experiences. Gilligan (2001) notes that the resilience literature emphasises the importance of diverse supports which may promote and sustain resilience.

Workers in contact with refugees and asylum-seekers should avoid denying or minimising the gravity of the traumatic events and processes to which their clients have been exposed. They should ensure that service users' voices are heard and challenge oppression, but combine this with the promotion of resilience :

helping the person to hang on to and build on positive factors, threads and niches in their lives, tapping into the commitment of strong elements in the .. social network. (Gilligan, 2001 : 7).

Workers can help service users to build new social networks through identifying ordinary but valued features of their lives, such as faith and religion, sports, talents, skills and interests, and actively linking service users to relevant services, clubs, and groups both inside and outside the refugee communities.

As Ireland becomes a truly multicultural society, and as diversity in ways of being becomes the norm rather than the exception, the challenge for us as workers is to find a way to combine sensitive and meaningful responsiveness to individual service users with advocacy at a more public level in pursuit of social equality and inclusion.

Cultural differences can only be freely elaborated and democratically mediated on the basis of social equality. (Fraser,1989 : 207, cited in Rossiter, 2000).

CHAPTER SIX

RESOURCE ORGANISATIONS

This section contains a list of statutory and voluntary organisations, which provide a range of advice, information and support resources for refugees and asylum seekers. They are also a resource for social workers and agencies, who are seeking information about particular communities or countries of origin, culturally specific advice, and contact with members of particular communities.

While every effort has been made to ensure that the information listed is accurate, any such list is soon out of date. We hope that organisations which are not listed or whose contact information changes can be located through contact with one of the other organisations.

Organisations

Access Ireland Refugee Social Integration Project
Richmond Business Campus
North Brunswick Street, Dublin 7
Tel: (01) 8780589
Fax: (01) 8780591
Email: accessireland@connect.ie

African Cultural Project
Ulster Bank Chambers
4 Lower O'Connell Street, Dublin 1
Tel: (01) 8780613
Fax: (01) 8780615

African Refugee Network
90 Meath Street, Dublin 8
Tel: (01) 4734523
Fax: (01) 4540745

Amnesty International
48 Fleet Street, Temple Bar, Dublin 2
Tel: (01) 6776361
Fax: (01) 6776392
Email: info@amnesty.iol.ie

Association of Refugees and Asylum Seekers in Ireland
213 North Circular Road, Dublin 7
Tel: (01) 8381142
Fax: (01) 8381143
Email: arasi@indigo.ie

Bosnian Community Development Project
40 Pearse Street, Dublin 2
Tel/Fax: (01) 6719202
Email: bcdp@iol.ie

Clann Housing Association
(Assistance in the provision of housing)
Floor 3, 18 Dame Street, Dublin 2
Tel: (01) 6775010

Comhlamh
10 Upper Camden Street, Dublin 2
Tel: (01) 4783490
Fax: (01) 4783738

Comhlamh
55 Grand Parade, Cork
Tel: 021 275881
Fax: 021 275241

Department of Education and Science
Marlborough Street, Dublin 1
Tel: (01) 8734700

Department of Justice, Equality and Law Reform
72 St. Stephen's Green, Dublin 2
Tel: (01) 6028202
Fax: (01) 6615461
Asylum (Policy)
Tel: (01) 6028202
Fax: (01) 6028532

Department of Social Community and Family Affairs
Aras Mhic Dhiarmada
Store Street, Dublin 1
Tel: (01) 8748444

Dublin Corporation
Civic Offices
Wood Quay, Dublin 8
Tel: (01) 6722222

Eastern Regional Health Authority
Head Office
Palmerstown, Dublin 20
Tel: (01) 4065600
Fax: (01) 4065601
Email: erha@erha.ie

Equality Authority
Clonmel Street, Dublin 2
Tel: (01) 4173333
Fax: (01) 4173366

Equality Investigations
Clonmel Street, Dublin 2
Tel: (01) 4173300
Fax: (01) 4173399

FAS Training Authority
Head Office
27/33 Baggot Street, Dublin 4
Tel: (01) 6070500
Fax: (01) 6070611

FLAC
Free Legal Advice Centres
49 South William Street, Dublin 2
Tel: (01) 6794239
Fax: (01) 6791554

Focus Ireland
14a Eustace Street, Dublin 1
Tel: (01) 6712555
Fax: (01) 6796843
Email: info@focusireland.ie

INTERACT IRELAND
(Access to employment for refugees)
Abbey House
15-17 Upper Abbey Street, Dublin 1
Tel: (01) 8747099

Irish Council for Civil Liberties
Dominick Court, 40-41 Lower Dominick Street, Dublin 1
Tel: (01) 8783136
Fax: (01) 8783109
Email: iccl@iol.ie

Irish Council for International Students (ICOS)
41 Morehampton Road, Dublin 4
Tel: (01) 6605233
Fax: (01) 6682320
Email: office@icosirl.iol.ie

Irish Episcopal Commission for Emigrants
57 Parnell Square West, Dublin 1
Tel: (01) 8723655

Irish Red Cross
16 Merrion Square, Dublin 2
Tel: (01) 6765135
Fax: (01) 6614461
Email: redcross@iol.ie

Irish Refugee Council
40 Lower Dominick Street, Dublin 1
Tel: (01) 8730042/8782854/8724424
Fax: (01) 8730088
Email: refugee@iol.ie

Irish Refugee Council
1 Bank Place, Ennis, Co Clare
Tel/Fax: (065) 682 2026
Fax: (065) 6822017
Email: irc.ennis@tinet.ie

Islamic Centre Dublin
163 South Circular Road, Dublin 8
Tel: (01) 4533242

Islamic Cultural Centre
19 Roebuck Road, Clonskeagh
Dublin 14
Tel: (01) 2603740

National Consultative Committee on Racism and Interculturalism
26 Harcourt Street, Dublin 2
Tel: (01) 4785777
Fax: (01) 4785778

Platform Against Racism
C/o Pavee Point
46 North Great Charles Street, Dublin 1
Tel: (01) 8780255
Email: pavee@iol.ie

Psychology Service for Refugees and Asylum Seekers
St Brendan's Hospital
Grangegorman, Dublin 7
Tel: (01) 8680166

Reception and Integration Agency (formerly the Refugee Agency)
9 Marlborough Court , Dublin
Tel: (01) 8787200
Fax: (01) 8787232

Refugee Applications Centre
Timberley House
79-83 Lower Mount Street, Dublin 2
Case Processing
Tel: (01) 6028116/6028063
Fax: (01) 6028127
Appeals
Tel: (01) 6028008
Fax: (01) 6028120
Administration
Tel: (01) 6028054
Fax: (01) 6028125

Refugee Information Service
Richmond Business Campus
North Brunswick Street, Dublin 2
Tel: (01) 8090437
Fax: (01) 8780591
Email: refinfo@eircom.net

Refugee Language Support Unit
83 Waterloo Lane, Dublin 4
Tel: (01) 6672479
Fax: (01) 6672355
Email: info@rlsunits.com

Refugee Medical Unit
Timberley House
79-83 Lower Mount Street, Dublin 2
Tel: (01) 6028167

SORUSI
Society of Russian Speakers of Ireland
C/o SICCDA
90 Meath Street, Dublin 8
Tel: (01) 4734758

Tallaght Refugee Support Service
West Tallaght Resource Centre
17 Glenshane Close, Tallaght, Dublin 24
Tel: (01) 4522486/4522533
Fax: (01) 4621740

Threshold
Housing Advice and Research Centre
19 Mary's Abbey, Dublin 7
Tel: (01) 8726311

Trinity College Dublin
Centre for Language and Communication Studies
ARTS Building, Trinity College, Dublin 2
Tel: (01) 6082184

United Nations High Commission for Refugees (UNHCR)
27 Fitzwilliam Street Upper, Dublin 2
Tel; (01) 6328675/79
Fax: (01) 6328676
Email: iredu@unhcr.ch

Vietnamese Irish Centre
45 Hardwicke Street, Dublin 1
Tel: (01) 8742331

Vincentian Refugee Centre
St Peter's Church
Phibsboro, Dublin 7
Tel: (01) 8389708
Fax: (01) 8389950
Email: refugeecentrephibsboro@eircom.net

Women's Refugee Project
West Tallaght Resource Centre
17 Glenshane Close, Tallaght, Dublin 24
Tel: (01) 4522486/4522533
Fax: (01) 4621740

Support Groups

contactable via Comhlamh, 10 Upper Camden Street, Dublin 2 – as above

African Association 2000

Africa Consortium

Algeria Solidarity Group

Anti-Racism Campaign

Association of Nigerian Asylum Seekers in Ireland (ANASI)

Bhutanes Refugee Support Group

Burma Action Ireland

CII (Communaute Ivoirienne en Irlande)

Congo Solidarity Group

Dublin Local Group of Survival International

Ireland Action for Bosnia

Irish Black and Migrant Women's Association

Irish Sudanese Solidarity Group

Kosovar Ireland Solidarity

Kurdistan Information Network

Middle East Solidarity Group

Pan African Organisation Limited

Residents against Racism

Romanian Community Group

Somali Community in Ireland

BIBLIOGRAPHY

Al-Rasheed, M. (1993), 'The meaning of marriage and status in exile. The experience of Iraqi women'. *Journal of Refugee Studies,* 6 (2) : 89 104

Bates, S. (1998), 'Tribunal jails Croat for new war crime of rape, *The Guardian, December 12.*

Bissland, J. and Lawand, K. (1997), 'Report of the UNHCR symposium on gender-based persecution 22-23 February 1996'. *International Journal of Refugee Law, Special Edition, Autumn : 11-32.*

Bloch, A., Galvin, T. and Harrell-Bond, B. (2000), 'Refugee women, children and families in Europe'. *International Migration Review, 38 (2).*

Burnett, A. and Peel, M. (2001), 'Health needs of asylum-seekers and refugees'. *British Medical Journal,* 322: 544-547.

Byrne, R. (1997), 'On the sliding scales of justice: the status of asylum seekers and refugees in Ireland', in Byrne, R. and Duncan, W. (eds.), *Developments in Discrimination Law in Ireland and Europe.* Dublin: Irish Centre for European Law, Trinity College Dublin.

Casey, S. and O'Connell, M. (2000), 'Pain and prejudice: assessing the experience of racism in Ireland', in McLachlan, M. and O'Connell, M. (eds.), *Cultivating Pluralism: psychological, social and cultural perspectives on a changing Ireland.* Dublin: Oak Tree Press.

Castles, S. and Miller, M.J. (1998), *The Age of Migration. London: Macmillan Press.*

Chau, K. (1990), 'A model for teaching cross-cultural practice in social work'. *Journal of Social Work Education,* 26 (2) : 124 - 133.

Cullen, P. (2000), *Refugees and Asylum-Seekers in Ireland.* Cork: Cork University Press.

Dalrymple, J. and Burke, B. (1995), *Anti-oppressive Practice: social care and the law.* Buckingham: Open University Press.

Dominelli, L. (1988), *Anti-Racist Social Work.* London: Macmillan Press / B.A.S.W.

Dominelli, L. (1997), *Anti-Racist Social Work.* Second edition. London: Macmillan Press / B.A.S.W.

Dominelli, L. (1998), 'Multiculturalism, anti-racism and social work', in Williams,C., Soydan, H., and Johnson, M. (eds.) *Social Work and Minorities: European perspectives.* London: Routledge.

Duffy, C. (1994), 'Female poverty, powerlessness and social exclusion in Ireland'. *Administration,* 42 (1) : 47 - 66.

Eastmond, M. (1993), 'Life: Chilean refugee women and the dilemmas of exile', in Buijs, G. (ed), *Migrant Women: crossing boundaries and changing identities.* Oxford: Berg.

Egan, S. and Costello, K. (1999), *Refugee Law Comparative Study.* Dublin: Faculty of Law, University College Dublin.

Ellegaard, M. (1997), *A Conference Report on Gender Related Persecution.* Copenhagen: Danish Refugee Council.

Essed, P. (1996), *Diversity: Gender, Color and Culture.* Amherst: University of Massachusetts Press.

Ewalt, P., Freeman, E., Kirk, S. and Poole, D. (eds.) (1996), *Multicultural Issues in Social Work..* Washington: NASW Press.

Faughnan, P. (1999), *Refugees and Asylum-Seekers in Ireland.* Dublin: Social Science Research Centre, University College Dublin.

Fook, J. (2000), 'Deconstructing and reconstructing professional expertise', in Fawcett, B., Featherstone, B., Fook, J. and Rossiter, A. (eds.), *Practice and Research in Postmodern Feminist Perspectives.* London: Routledge.

Fozzard, S. (1987), 'Life in Limbo. Vietnamese refugees in the closed centres of Hong Kong', *Third World Affairs* : 348-351

Fraser, N. (1989), *Unruly Practices: power, discourse and gender in contemporary social theory.* Minneapolis: University of Minnesota Press.

Fuglerud, O. (1997), 'Ambivalent incorporation: Norwegian policy towards Tamil asylum-seekers from Sri Lanka', *Journal of Refugee Studies,* 10 (4).

Galvin, T. (2000), 'Refugee Status in Exile: the case of African asylum-seekers in Ireland' in MacLachlan, M. and O' Connell, M. (eds.), *Cultivating Pluralism.* Dublin: Oaktree Press.

Gambe, D., Gomes, J., Kapur, V., Rangel, M., and Stubbs, P. (1992), *Antiracist Social Work Education, 2: Improving Practice with Children and Families: a training manual.* London: C.C.E.T.S.W.

Gilligan, R. (2001), *Promoting Resilience.* London: B.A.A.F.

Government of Ireland (1996), *Refugee Act.* Dublin : Stationery Office.

Hanlon, H. (2000), 'Asylum upsurge due to mounting violations of rights'. *The Irish Times, May 20.*

Harrell-Bond, B. (1986), *Imposing Aid.* Oxford: Oxford University Press.

Harrell-Bond, B. (1999), 'The experience or refugees as recipients of aid', in Ager, A. (ed), *Refugees: perspectives on the experience of forced migration.* London: Cassell.

Haughey, N. (2001), 'Children in a state of exile'. *The Irish Times, February 9.*

Hirschon, R. (1989), *Heirs of the Greek Catastrophe: the social life of Asia Minor refugees in Piraeus.* Oxford: Clarendon Press.

Horgan, O. (2000), "Seeking refuge in Ireland: acculturation stress and perceived discrimination', in McLachlan, M. and O'Connell, M. (eds.), *Cultivating Pluralism: psychological, social and cultural perspectives on a changing Ireland.* Dublin: Oak Tree Press.

I.F.S.W. (1996), *Fighting Exclusion: Social Work in Action.* Promotional leaflet.

Johnson, M., Baldwin-Edwards, M. and Moraes, C. (1998), 'Controls, rights and migration', in Williams, C., Soydan, H., and Johnson, M. (eds.), *Social Work with Minorities.* London: Routledge.

Joly, D., Nettleton, C., and Poulton, H. (1992), *Refugees : Asylum in Europe.* London: Minority Rights Publications.

Joly, D. (1996), *Haven or Hell? Asylum Policies and Refugees in Europe.* London: Macmillan Press

Kay, D. and Miles, R. (1992), *Refugees or Migrant Workers? European Volunteer Workers in Britain 1946-1951.* London: Routledge.

Krause, I. B. (1998), *Therapy Across Culture.* London: Sage

Lentin, R. (ed.)(1998), *The Expanding Nation: towards a multi-ethnic Ireland: Conference Papers. Dublin: Department of Sociology,* Trinity College Dublin

Levy, S. (1999), 'Containment and validation: psychodynamic insights into refugees' experience of torture', in Alger, A.(ed.), *Refugees: perspectives on the experience of forced migration.* London: Cassell.

Loescher, Gil and Scanlan, John A. (1985), *Calculated Kindness: refugees and America's half-open door, 1945 to the present.* New York: Free Press.

Mallon, G. (1998) 'Knowledge for Practice with Gay and Lesbian Persons', in Mallon, G. (ed.) *Foundations of Social Work Practice with Lesbian and Gay Persons.* New York: Haworth Press.

Marx, E. (1990), 'The social world of refugees: a conceptual framework'. *Journal of Refugee Studies,* 3 (3).

Maslow, A.H. (1970), *Motivation and Personality. Second edition.* New York: Harper and Row.

Mattaini, M. (1995), 'Knowledge for practice', in Meyer, C. and Mattaini, M. (eds.), *Foundations of Social Work Practice.* Washington, D.C: N.A.S.W.

McGovern, F. (1990), *Vietnamese Refugees in Ireland, 1979 to 1989. A case study in resettlement and education.* Unpublished M.Ed. thesis. Dublin: Trinity College Dublin.

McKay, S. (2000), 'They look for Justice. Sadly they don't find it'. *The Sunday Tribune. June 11.*

Northern Ireland Women's Aid Federation (1998), *Violence on the Edge: exploring the needs of minority ethnic women at risk of domestic violence in Northern Ireland.* Northern Ireland Women's Aid Federation / Training for Women Network Ltd.

O.E.C.D. (1995), *Trends in International Migration: Annual Report 1994.* Paris: OECD

O'Regan, C. (1998), *Report of a Survey of the Vietnamese and Bosnian Refugee Communities in Ireland.* Dublin: Refugee Agency. Refugee Resettlement Research Project.

O'Regan, C. (2000), 'Immigration and resettlement in Ireland: planning services, supporting people', in MacLachlan, M. and O'Connell, M. (eds.), *Cultivating Pluralism: psychological, social and cultural perspectives on a changing Ireland.* Dublin: Oak Tree Press

O'Sullivan, E. (1997), *Homelessness. Housing Need and Asylum Seekers in Ireland - a report for the Homeless Initiative.* Dublin: Homeless Initiative.

Payne, M. (1997), *Modern Social Work Theory.* Second edition. London: Macmillan Press.

Potocky, M. (1997) Multicultural social work in the United States: a review and critique. *International Social Work,* 40 : 315-326.

Powell, F. (1995) Citizenship and Social Exclusion. *Administration, 43 (3) : 22-35.*

Refugee Agency (1997), *Information Bulletin.* Dublin.

Refugee Agency (1997), *Annual Report.* Dublin.

Refugee Agency (1998), *Annual Report.* Dublin.

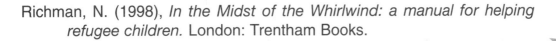

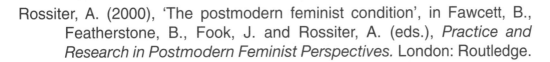

Richman, N. (1998), *In the Midst of the Whirlwind: a manual for helping refugee children.* London: Trentham Books.

Ronnau, J. (1994), 'Teaching cultural competence: practical ideas for social work educators'. *Journal of Multicultural Social Work 3* (1) : 29-42.

Rossiter, A. (2000), 'The postmodern feminist condition', in Fawcett, B., Featherstone, B., Fook, J. and Rossiter, A. (eds.), *Practice and Research in Postmodern Feminist Perspectives.* London: Routledge.

Sansani, 1 (2001), *The Provision of Health Services in Ireland to Refugee Women who have Survived Gender-Based Torture.* Unpublished M.Phil. thesis. Dublin: Department of Sociology, Trinity College, Dublin

Scottish Office (1998), *Valuing Diversity: having regard to the racial, religious, cultural and linguistic needs of Scotland's children.* Edinburgh: Social Work Services Inspectorate.

Separated Children in Europe Programme (1999), *Statement of Good Practice.* Geneva: U.N.H.C.R. / Save the Children Alliance.

Shipsey, B. (1994), 'Immigration law and refugees', in Heffernan, L. (ed.), *Human Rights: a European perspective.* Dublin: The Round Hall Press.

Skehill, C (1999), *The Nature of Social Work in Ireland: a historical perspective.* Lewiston, New York: The Edwin Mellen Press.

Smith, T. (1997), 'Racist encounters: Romani 'Gypsy' women and mainstream health services'. *The European Journal of Women's Studies,* 4 (2) : 183-196.

Summerfield, D. (1996), *The Impact of War and Atrocity on Civilian Populations: basic principles for N.G.O. interventions and a critique of psychosocial trauma projects.* London: Relief and Rehabilitation Network, Overseas Development Institute.

Thompson, N. (1993), *Anti-Discriminatory Practice.* London: Macmillan Press / B.A.S.W.

Thompson, N. (1997), *Anti-Discriminatory Practice.* Second edition. London: Macmillan Press / B.A.S.W.

United Nations (UN) (1987), Human Rights: questions and answers. New York: U.N.

United Nations Centre for Human Rights (1994), *Human Rights and Social Work – a manual for schools of social work and the social work profession.* New York: United Nations Centre for Human Rights.

U.N.H.C.R. (1991), *Guidelines on the Protection of Refugee Women.* Geneva.

U.N.H.C.R. web site: http://www.unhcr.ch/

Vace, N., deVaney, S. and Wittmer, J. (1995), *Experiencing and Counselling Multicultural and Diverse Populations.* Third edition. Bristol, PA: Accelerated development Publishers.

Waldron, S. (1988), 'Working in the dark. Why social anthropological research is essential in refugee administration'. *Journal of Refugee Studies,* 1 (2) :153-165.

Ward, E. (1996), 'A big show-off to show what we could do' – Ireland and the Hungarian refugee crisis of 1956'. *Irish Studies in International Affairs,* 7 :131-141

Ward, E. (1998), 'Ireland and refugees/asylum seekers: 1922 –1996' in Lentin, R. (ed.), *The Expanding Nation: towards a multi-ethnic Ireland: Conference Papers.* Dublin: Department of Sociology, Trinity College Dublin

Ward, D. (2000), 'Welcome here: how the threat of deportation changed two schools forever', *The Guardian. Education Supplement.* November 21.

Witkin, S. (1998), 'Human rights and social work'. *Social Work,* 43 (3) : 197-201.

Zetter, R. (1988), 'Refugees and Refugee Studies: a label and an agenda'. *Journal of Refugee Studies,* 1 (1) : 1-6.

Zetter, R. (1991), 'Labelling refugees: forming and transforming a bureaucratic identity'. *Journal of Refugee Studies,* 4 (1).